1st International Workshop on Multilingual, Multimodal and Multitask Language Generation (Mutli3Generation)

Tampere, Finland
15 June 2023

ISBN: 978-1-7138-8997-7

Printed from e-media with permission by:

Curran Associates, Inc.
57 Morehouse Lane
Red Hook, NY 12571

Some format issues inherent in the e-media version may also appear in this print version.

Printed with permission by Curran Associates, Inc. (2024)

For permission requests, please contact the Association for Computational Linguistics at the address below.

Association for Computational Linguistics
209 N. Eighth Street
Stroudsburg, Pennsylvania 18360

Phone: 1-570-476-8006
Fax: 1-570-476-0860

acl@aclweb.org

Additional copies of this publication are available from:

Curran Associates, Inc.
57 Morehouse Lane
Red Hook, NY 12571 USA
Phone: 845-758-0400
Fax: 845-758-2633
Email: curran@proceedings.com
Web: www.proceedings.com

Multi3Generation 2023

Proceedings of the 1st International Workshop on Multilingual, Multimodal and Multitask Language Generation (Multi3Generation)

15 June, 2023
Tampere University
Tampere, Finland

Order copies of this and other ACL proceedings from:

Association for Computational Linguistics (ACL)
209 N. Eighth Street
Stroudsburg, PA 18360
USA
Tel: +1-570-476-8006
Fax: +1-570-476-0860
acl@aclweb.org

Introduction

Welcome to the 1st edition of the International International Workshop on Multilingual, Multimodal and Multitask Language Generation (Multi3Generation) in Tampere, Finland. The aim of Multi3Generation is to bring together researchers interested in any aspects of language generation and its derived applications, such as machine translation, text summarisation, text simplification, description generation, etc., especially focusing on multilingual, multimodal and multitask aspects.

The Action embraces both symbolic and machine learning approaches to Natural Language Generation (NLG), and everything in between. This is reflected in the talks of the session. The programme includes research works which relate to: i) language resources and representation, including multilingual paraphrasing and interlingual representations; ii) machine translation, taking into account Polish and Ukranian languages; and iii) language generation, addressing specific challenges or domains.

The talk of our keynote speaker, Prof. André Martins, also reflect these themes. His work focuses on NLP explainability and multilinguality.

We include the abstract of each talk in this volume. In total, we accepted 7 long papers following the recommendations of our peer reviewers. We are extremely grateful to the Programme Committee members for their detailed and helpful reviews. The papers will be presented as talks.

The workshop session was organised in a way to allow time for discussion after each talk to allow participants to initiate debate over the presented papers, and thus, over the language generation topic.

Multi3Generation 2023 has received financial support (covering over a half of the costs) from the COST Action "Multi3Generation: Multi-task, Multilingual, Multi-modal Language Generation" (CA18231).

We very much hope that you will have an enjoyable and inspiring time!

Anabela Barreiro, Elena Lloret & Max Silberztein

Lisbon, Alicante & Besançon

June 2023

Organisers:

Workshop organisers:
Anabela Barreiro (INESC-ID Lisboa, Portugal),
Max Silberztein (University of Franche-Comté, France)
Elena Lloret (University of Alicante, Spain)
Proceedings chair:
Max Silberztein (Université de Franche-Comté, France)
Web and dissemination chair:
Marcin Paprzycki (Systems Research Institute Polish Academy of Sciences, Poland)

Program Committee:

- Mirela Alhasani (EPOKA University, Albania)
- Isabelle Augenstein (University of Copenhagen, Denmark)
- Mehul Bhatt (Örebro University, Sweden)
- Anabela Barreiro (INESC-ID Lisboa, Portugal) Iacer Calixto (Universiteit van Amsterdam, Netherlands)
- José Camargo (Unbabel, Portugal)
- Liviu Dinu (University of Bucharest, Romania)
- Aykut Erdem (Koç University, Turkey)
- Maria Ganzha (Warsaw University of Technology, Poland)
- Albert Gatt (Universiteit Utrecht, Netherlands)
- Fabio Kepler (Unbabel, Portugal)
- Elena Lloret (University of Alicante, Spain)
- Helena Moniz (University of Lisboa and INESC-ID Lisboa, Portugal)
- Marcin Paprzycki (Systems Research Institute Polish Academy of Sciences, Poland)
- Max Silberztein (University of Franche-Comté, France)
- Inguna Skadina (University of Latvia, Latvia)
- Irene Russo (ILC CNR, Italy)
- Oleksii Turuta (Kharkiv National University of Radio Electronics – NURE, Ukraine)

Invited Speaker:

André Martins, Instituto Superior Técnico, University of Lisbon.

Invited Talk

André Martins: Towards Explainable and Reliable Multilingual NLP

Natural language processing systems are becoming increasingly accurate and powerful. However, in order to take full advantage of these advances, new capabilities are necessary for humans to understand model predictions and when to question or to bypass them. In this talk, I will present recent work from our group in two directions.

In the first part, I will describe a new approach for selective rationalization based on sparse and structured transformations (sparsemax, alpha-entmax, and LP-SparseMAP), all drop-in replacements for softmax that permit handling constraints through differentiable layers. This leads to SPECTRA, a deterministic and structured rationalizer with favorable properties in terms of predictive power, quality of the explanations, and model variability. Then, I will present CREST (ContRastive Edits with Sparse raTionalization), which combines the above idea with a counterfactual text generator, leading to improvements in counterfactual quality, model robustness, and interpretability. We introduce a new loss function that leverages CREST counterfactuals to regularize selective rationales using SPECTRA and show that this regularization improves both model robustness and rationale quality, compared to methods that do not leverage CREST counterfactuals.

In the second part, I will present several methods for detecting and correcting hallucinations in neural machine translation (NMT). We annotate a dataset of over 3.4k sentences indicating different kinds of critical errors and hallucinations. We compare several detection methods, both glass-box uncertainty-based detectors and model-based detectors. As hallucinations are detached from the source content, they exhibit encoder-decoder attention patterns that are statistically different from those of good quality translations. We frame this problem with an optimal transport formulation and propose a fully unsupervised, plug-in detector that can be used with any attention-based NMT model. Finally, we study hallucinations in massively multilingual models by conducting a comprehensive analysis on both the M2M family of conventional neural machine translation models and ChatGPT / GPT-4. Our investigation covers a broad spectrum of conditions, spanning over 100 translation directions across various resource levels and going beyond English-centric language pairs. We provide key insights regarding the prevalence, properties, and mitigation of hallucinations, paving the way towards more responsible and reliable machine translation systems.

This is joint work with Marcos Treviso, Nuno Guerreiro, Duarte Alves, Vlad Niculae, Ben Peters, Pierre Colombo, Alexis Ross, Elena Voita, Jonas Waldendorf, Barry Haddow, Alexandra Birch, Pablo Piantanida in the scope of the DeepSPIN, MAIA, and UTTER projects.

Table of Contents

Controllability for English-Ukrainian Machine Translation Based on Specialized Corpora

Daniil Maksymenko, Olena Turuta, Nataliia Saichyshyna, Maksym Yerokhin and Oleksii Turuta
Kharkiv National University of Radio Electronics / Nauky Ave. 14, Kharkiv, Ukraine
{daniil.maksymenko, olena.turuta, nataliia.saichyshyna, oleksii.turuta}@nure.ua

Abstract

Significant difficulty in translation tasks is usually caused by the possibility of having multiple correct results. That is where human translators usually beat modern machine learning models, as they have much more external context, which can be useful to create a correct translation both from the meaning and style sides.

The purpose of this article is to provide a possible solution for the lack of context during machine translation, which would provide an ability to increase the controllability of existing machine translation architectures. We propose a new architecture, which would incorporate this additional embedded context into the translation and compare this new approach to some classic ones like just transfer learning of some new features using an existing, trained model.

We conducted some experiments using the proposed architecture to check if it indeed allows controlling of the translation process and measured the new model using both token and embedding metrics.

1 Introduction

Usage of encoder-decoder architecture with different approaches like LSTMs or transformers allowed for achieving human-like translation (Sutskever et al., 2014). However, such models still cannot outperform professional translators with years of experience. Models can capture meaning, and they can translate some difficult terms or even ones they did not see during training, but usually, they work with a black box approach, when we just provide input text and wait for the result.

The most classic approach to change the model and its behavior is to make some fine-tuning or apply transfer learning to some existing architectures (Kocmi, 2020). However, we need a good dataset to make it work and tuning can take a long time, depending on the amount of available data, model size, and hardware.

Text generation models like T5, which can also be used for translation, allow us to add some special tokens or just descriptions of style or sentiment (Raffel et al., 2022). This approach should work well without any fine-tuning, as it is based on the zero-shot learning concept (Xian et al., 2018). However, a special token or short description can be not enough to significantly alter the result of the model. This method works much better with recent models like GPT 3 or ChatGPT, but they are available only as APIs and still make many errors in any other language than English, as they were trained for it originally (Brown et al., 2020). Some solutions propose adding a topic modeling result into the translation, but it also does not provide too many opportunities to affect the model (Eidelman et al., 2012).

In this work, we propose an architecture to get better controllability over the machine translation tasks by adding some external context in there, which can be obtained from another model. We provide examples of how our approach works, show the theory behind it, and provide some ideas for further development in this area. New architecture gets measured with both token and embedding metrics. It should be compared with some machine translation models trained during our previous research with the usage of transfer learning, so we can check if this new concept works better than the classic one.

2 Datasets

In the process of preparing the study, we reviewed, downloaded, and analyzed a large number of existing datasets for the Ukrainian language. Moreover, here we used datasets prepared and collected earlier by ourselves, which also contributed to the results. We paid attention to the collected data, its analysis, cleaning, and checking the accuracy since the data directly affects the results of the task. In addition, when solving the controllability problem, we must be sure that the data is unambiguously related to the declared domain. Four specific domains were collected, which are described below.

- **Common texts** compiled on the basis of the manual translation of the Multi30k dataset (Elliott et al., 2016). Covers general topics.
- **Scientific articles** are sufficiently large and informative translations of scientific articles with the appropriate scientific style.
- **Ukrainian laws** are certified translations of legislation intended for foreign organizations. The style of the texts is official.
- **Technical documentation** is guidelines for using a web application programming framework

The collection process and more information are described in the previous article (Maksymenko et al., 2022). The domains were chosen in such a way that they have distinctive styles of texts and the controllability of the resulting translations can be clearly traced.

In addition to the texts described above, which have an explicit style, we trained our model using large datasets for the Ukrainian language. These include OPUS datasets that contain datasets of hundreds of thousands of lines, but do not guarantee the correctness and exact correspondence of the English and Ukrainian translations (Zhang et al., 2020a). Because of this, the preparation of these datasets involved checking the cosine similarity, determining the source language, and more.

Initial processing means filtering out duplicates, empty lines, lines with incorrect values in the form of characters that do not carry semantic value. After that, the resulting sentences were processed using distiluse-base-multilingual-cased-v2 (Reimers and Gurevych, 2019) multilingual model in order to calculate the cosine similarity of strings to compare their identity in meaning. In this way, we were able to clean the existing datasets from mistranslations, "shifted lines" and semantic errors. A value of 0.4 was chosen as the threshold value for cosine similarity, which is considered sufficient to maintain semantic similarity between sentences. We also examined sentences that were beyond the cosine similarity line of 0.4. In most cases, the sentences were screened out fairly, but there were also cases where the sentences were in a figurative sense and were also marked as incorrectly translated.

Such cases were found and were not excluded from the data sets, which gives us the opportunity to train the model to understand the figurative meaning. In this way, we prove that these metrics cannot be used as a standard benchmark, since they do not handle phraseological units and slang. We have achieved a large amount of clean data, which helped us to restore the decoder and became the basis for retraining the model on the specific domains described above.

3 Proposed solution

For the last decade translation models use an encoder-decoder architecture, which takes a vector of tokens, creates their embedding matrix, passes it through some recurrent or attention layers, and then creates a new vector of tokens from this original text embedding. As we mentioned before we can try to affect translation by using some special tokens to show the network the desired style or tone, but it does not give great results for controllability. Usually, good human translation is based on not only an understanding of both input and target languages but also on knowledge of a greater context of certain text, like having some good past examples, knowing events that are described in the text, and emotional and sentimental features in it. Modern neural translators can capture some of it by just getting fed with terabytes of data, but we still can not modify or tweak their understanding of the input. We can't interfere with the translation style without finetuning or we can just hope that adding some instruction or special tokens, will change the output of the model. A possible solution can be to use an idea proposed for instant voice transfer in text-to-speech tasks, like SV2TTS architecture (speaker verification to text-to-speech) (Jia et al., 2018)). This architecture uses an external model to create an embedding of the speaker's voice, which then gets merged with an embedding matrix of tokens sequence (each column of a matrix gets merged with this voice vector). This external model gets trained on some other tasks, like speaker verification, which allows it to learn necessary features, which can be transferred somewhere else later. We can use semantic search models in the case of machine translation as they learn the meaning and some stylistic features of texts, which allows us to put the original text in a vector space before translation and move it towards chosen domain in this space to change

Dataset name	Initial row count	Row count after initial processing	Row count after cos sim checking
OPUS-kde4-v2-eng-ukr	233 611	172 898	145 796
OPUS-multiccaligned-v1-eng-ukr	1 400 000	1 080 177	1 069 201
OPUS-opensubtitles-v2016-eng-ukr	612 127	486 564	427 355
OPUS-eubookshop-v2-eng-ukr	1790	725	497
Total	**2 247 528**	**1 740 364**	**1 642 849**

Table 1: OPUS datasets analysis.

	en	uk	cos_sim
739	I wish I was with you.	Шкода, що мене немає поруч.	0.21452248
13459	We're in the home stretch.	Ми на фінішній прямій.	0.23590076
23021	Tom is a nonagenarian.	Тому за дев'яносто.	0.20196614
27765	There's no use crying over spilled milk.	Зробленого не повернеш.	0.10168391
34401	Tomato, tomato.	Це одне й те саме.	0.14818832
41596	Well, it's horses for courses, isn't it?	Ну, кожному своє, еге ж?	0.20013674
44944	Give someone an inch, and they will take a mile.	Посади свиню за стіл, вона й ноги на стіл.	0.20188773

Figure 1: Figurative sentences

the output. Figure 2 shows us 2D projections of text embeddings obtained from Siamese BERT in miniLM implementation (Reimers and Gurevych, 2019). Here you can see how some texts start to form clouds based on topic, style, wording, and sentiment. For example, we can see how abstracts from scientific articles are getting close to some general texts, which can be explained by their attempt to describe something difficult with more casual terms to easily explain the main point of the article. Also, clouds for programming documentation and laws are distanced from all the other samples. Even within laws, we can see a few big groups, like laws that describe education or laws, which describe agreements. That can become a solution for the outer context problem in machine translation as we would provide not only tokens but also the position of the input text in this embedding plane described by the semantic and stylistic features vector. Also, we conducted some further research on these groups to prove that semantic search embeddings can be used to distinguish between different categories of texts, so we can affect the translation and help our network learn faster by using this external context. We created heatmaps of mean vectors for each category of texts to check how much they usually differ. In figure 3 you can see one small slice of this heatmap that shows how some parts of more serious texts like laws and acts tend to get more negative values. Their counterparts usually get higher values for the same features. Cases, where this distribution is opposite, are also possible, but all 4 vectors can still be distinguished well. Increasing or decreasing certain features in the initial embedding simultaneously to make it closer to some group of texts should allow us to save the original text features and add more information on a desired domain, style, and sentiment. For example, we put input text on the plane shown in Figure 2 among all the other texts. This text was used: "He came to the throne at the age of 73, an age when most people are thinking more about retirement than taking up a big and important job.". It falls somewhere between articles and general ones, as it is part of an article, but does not contain any specific words or stylistic features. We will try to move it to the laws-like domain so that the translation should get written in a more official language. In order to achieve it let's calculate the difference between each element of the input text vector and laws mean embedding. Then we will multiply these differences by a coefficient, which can be called a transformation power. It shows how much we want to move this text in a certain cluster

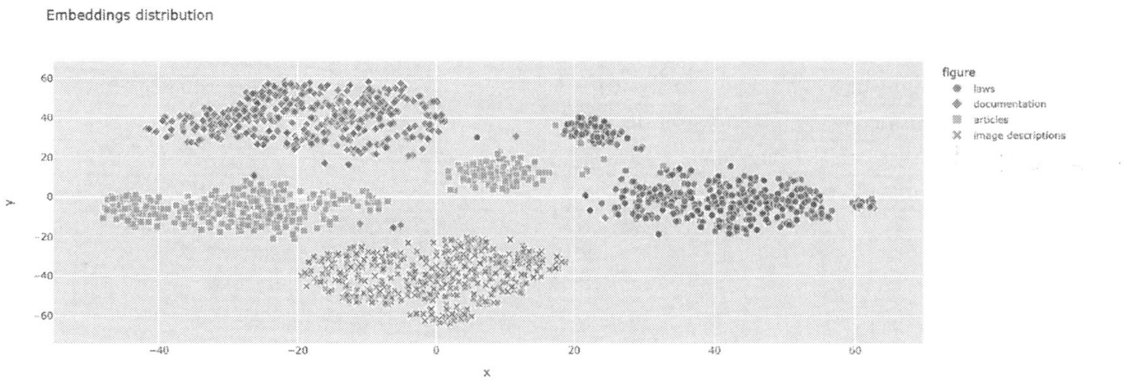

Figure 2: 2D projections of text embeddings.

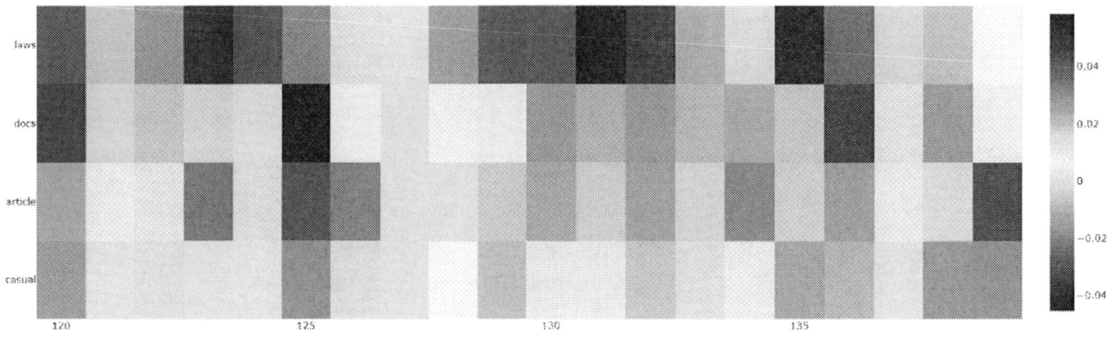

Figure 3: Slice of a heatmap of category mean embeddings

and how many changes should we apply to the original vector. Finally, we will subtract this multiplied vector of differences from the original embedding to create a new embedding skewed into a certain domain space. In figure 4 we show how the original text embedding (big yellow cross) gets moved into laws space more and more as we increase the transformation power by 1 starting with 1.5 (big bright blue circles are laws-transformed original text embeddings).

So our theory is that usage of semantic search embeddings should allow getting more control over the way the encoder-decoder model translates a text by showing it what the desired domain in a certain case.

4 Model architecture

We used huggingface transformers implementation of MarianMT as a basis for our model (Junczys-Dowmunt et al., 2018). It uses the BART interface and weights pretrained in the Marian C framework (Lewis et al., 2020). So original architecture can be described as an encoder-decoder model where both parts have 6 layers. Encoder can get up to 512 tokens and returns a matrix of embeddings with a dimension of 512x512. Siamese BERT in miniLM format was used in our modification to capture general text features. It gives us a vector with 384 values to describe a domain of the text, its meaning, and its style. This vector gets merged with each token embedding, so we get a matrix with a dimension of 512x896, which then gets reduced to the original 512x512 dimension using a fully-connected layer and SELU activation. This transformed matrix is used as an input for the decoder, so by modifying this semantic and stylistic embedding we can change the results of the model.

OpusMT English-to-Ukrainian model by Helsinki NLP was used as initial weights for the encoder and decoder in the modified architecture (Tiedemann and Thottingal, 2020).

5 Modified model training

Such a change of architecture would definitely affect the performance of the model and ruin the connection between the encoder and decoder, so the modified model would need massive tuning before further measurements and comparisons. In

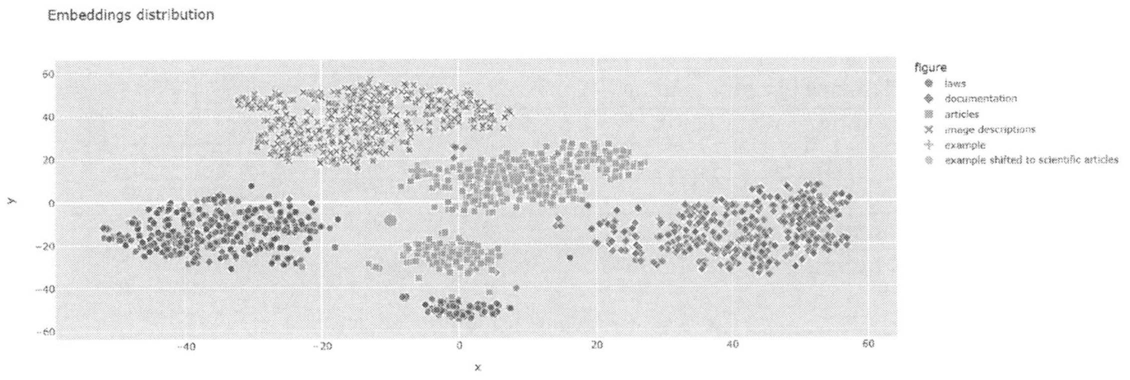

Figure 4: Example of shifting a text in a certain domain

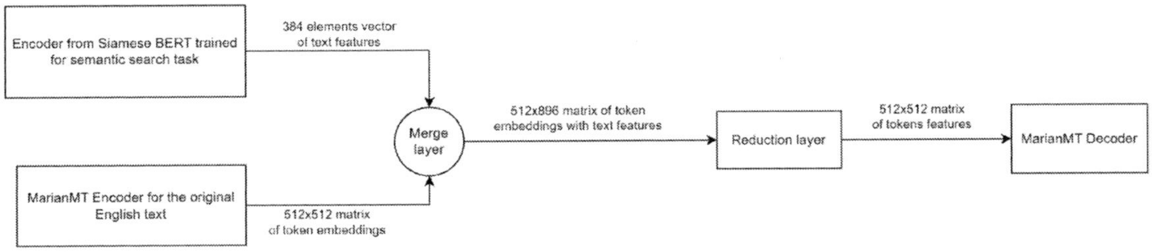

Figure 5: Modified MarianMT architecture with external context vectors

order to restore the encoder-decoder connection we trained the modified architecture using previously described datasets (2 million texts) on a single Nvidia T4 GPU for 5 epochs, which took us around 34 hours to complete. A subset of our gathered multidomain texts was used as a validation set to measure the validation loss and metrics (the subset contains 25% of all gathered texts from general, law, and scientific texts). The best epoch gets saved and it will be used in further experiments. We used token-based metrics like BLEU (Papineni et al., 2002) and METEOR (Banerjee and Lavie, 2005) to measure translation quality and embedding-based metric BERT Score (Zhang et al., 2020b) to check if translation possibly has the same meaning but uses a different set of words or text structure than the ground truth value. This way we can compare the new model with our previous research. Model fitting and restoration of performance can be seen in the table below, which shows metrics values on our custom validation subset:

One of the most interesting details here is that embedding metric BERT Score did not show how bad the performance really was after modifying MarianMT architecture and before fine-tuning when some old and proved token metrics showed how much progress did the model do in those 5 epochs of tuning. If we use only BERT Score to judge the model, then we will most likely think that the performance is not critically bad. However, here is one example of how a ruined connection between the encoder and decoder affected translation quality. Here is the original English text: "He has to come back in the next movie", which should be translated to Ukrainian as "Він має повернутися в наступному фільмі" . Modified MarianMT before fine-tuning gives a translation, which is absolutely not related to the original: "Це означає, що ми маємо справу з іншими людьми, а не з ними". We consider that the bad performance of the BERT Score was caused by the model beneath it. Metric uses English BERT for English texts and Multilingual BERT for any other language like Ukrainian. Model gets trained on 104 languages and it was proved multiple times that it performs much worse than language-specific models like UkrROBERTA (Panchenko et al., 2022). So probably BERT Score was still able to obtain some similar token-embedding pairs in ground-truth and wrongly translated texts and it was enough to give an average score, even if the model was absolutely wrong. This proves that embedding metrics are still not ready to be used as main performance measures for machine translation tasks. In order to

Model state	BLEU	METEOR	BERT Score F1
Original MarianMT before modification	11.20	0.2807	0.8115
Modified MarianMT without tuning	0.02	0.0147	0.5859
Epoch 1 of tuning	28.45	0.4387	0.8848
Epoch 2 of tuning	32.50	0.4627	0.8935
Epoch 3 of tuning	34.22	0.4730	0.8977
Epoch 4 of tuning	35.09	0.4781	0.8998
Epoch 5 of tuning	**36.14**	**0.4830**	**0.9021**

Table 2: Metrics values on our custom validation subset.

finally confirm that the modified architecture is ready for use we compared it to a set of individually finetuned MarianMT models from our previous research. They were tuned using our gathered texts to check if we can achieve controllability of translation style and domain with a small set of data for low-resource languages, so there are 3 models tuned with laws, scientific articles, and image descriptions separately and 1 model tuned with all these samples. The comparison was based on validation results on our subset of multidomain texts, so it proved that we were able to restore the performance of our best model from the previous research and even surpassed it. Measurements can be seen in the table below:

Such an architecture should also ease tuning for new domains, as we can try to distinguish them by placing a text on the semantic embeddings plane before translating it. Once the model regained its original performance and even improved it, we can move to the experiments on controllability to check our theory about additional context vectors.

6 Experiments description

Now we can take some texts, which can be interpreted in multiple ways, and try to translate them with some modifications of the embedding vector. We will take the text "Give my money back" as a first example, as it can be translated straight forward or in a more serious or even mean way. First of all, we will just translate the text using the tuned model. The result is "Поверни мені мої гроші" , which is a correct translation, which would work in most cases. Let's try to make it more serious and official. We will shift the embedding towards the laws text domain with transformation power equal to 1.5 in order to achieve it. New embedding allows us to get the following result: "Повертайте мої гроші назад". If we make the transformation power coefficient higher (like 5.5 for example) we can obtain the following results: "Повертайте мої гроші", which sounds like a short and official request. Also, we tried to move it closer to the documentation domain with coefficient 5.5, which gave us this output: "Віддати мої гроші". This translation does not look like something, which could be used in a real life, but it was still interesting to see how the network made the text sound like an instruction you could read in some manual. Here is the visualization of where the original embedding fell and where did the other vectors appear. Let's take a look at another example: "Then, about seven years after the gold rush began, it finished". Initially model gives a correct translation, which sounds like that: "Через сім років після початку золотої лихоманки все закінчилося". However, it lacks some stylistic features of the original text, but we can move the embedding closer to scientific articles to make it sound more like the original text. We will use transformation power equal to 3.5 and it gives this output: "Потім, близько семи років після початку золотої лихоманки, вона завершилася". This text sounds much closer to the English original than the first obtained one. Let's show how the text moves deeper into the scientific articles domain. One modified embedding has power equal to 1.5 and moves to the articles cloud and our final embedding with 3.5 power moves somewhere in between laws and articles, which allowed us to get a better translation in the end.

Even if the model did not get any historical documents or descriptions of historic documents, it was able to use features it learned in other domains to form some understanding of how provided text should be translated to become closer to those historical documents.

Here is one more example of how translation controllability works in our model. We have the following English text: "What are you going to

Model	BLEU	METEOR	BERT Score F1
Laws-only tuned MarianMT	25.34	0.3861	0.8630
Science-only tuned MarianMT	18.88	0.3347	0.8448
Descriptions-only tuned MarianMT	12.70	0.3034	0.8380
All texts tuned MarianMT	34.16	0.4754	0.8983
Modified MarianMT with context vector	**36.14**	**0.4830**	**0.9021**

Table 3: Performance of models.

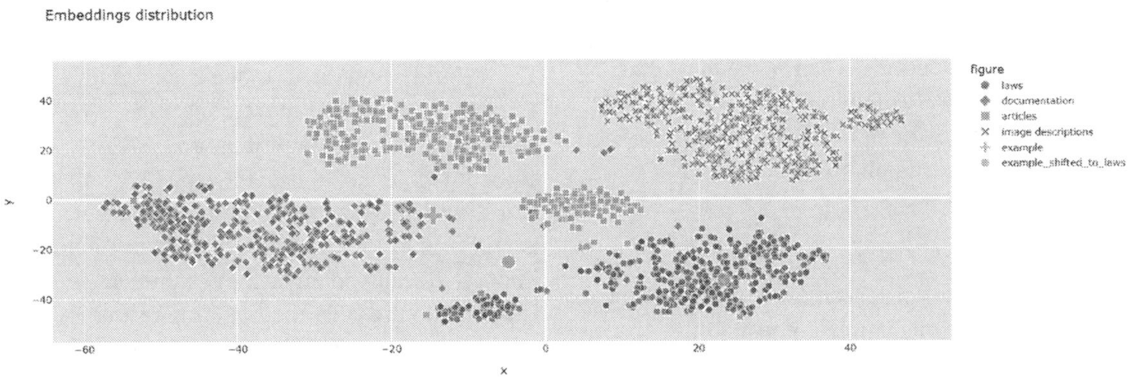

Figure 6: Change of the original text embedding towards laws

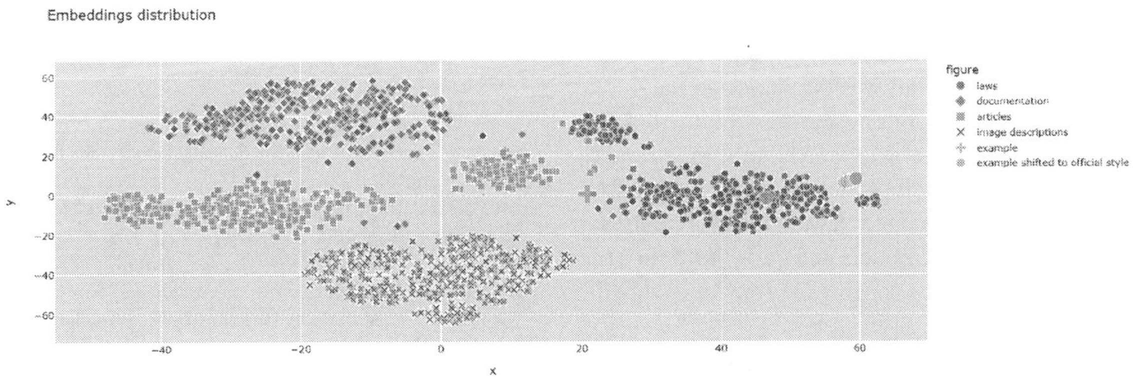

Figure 7: Text shifted to the scientific articles domain

eat with your sandwich?". It gets translated to Ukrainian like that: "Що ти їстимеш зі своїм бутербродом?". This translation is fine, but let's make it sound like a more modern speech (by moving it toward casual texts with power 6.5). The new text uses words, which are more expected from some modern kids and it sounds like that: "Що ти будеш їсти зі своїм сендвічем?". Not only did it change the translation of "sandwich", but it also changed the structure of the sentence to make it sound lighter.

So, this way we can make a translated text sound differently without some additional model finetuning or modifications. We just need to get a library of examples for different states, like historical texts, which use old words and phrases, laws, documentation, manuals, news, some jokes, or casual dialogues. Mean embedding vectors should be calculated for these categories. Then we can move a text feature vector toward chosen cluster and the model output should become more like it, which we were able to do in the examples above.

7 Conclusion

In this research we proposed a solution to achieve better machine translation controllability by ingesting some external context into the original text tokens embeddings. We modified MarianMT encoder-decoder architecture to combine the embedding matrix with a semantic search embedding vector of the original text to add more information about style, meaning, and sentiment. The new model was tuned to regain its original performance using 2 million texts from OPUS datasets and our own scrapped sets, which consist of multi30k image descriptions, laws translations, scientific articles abstracts, and programming framework documentation. The model was compared to the ones trained in our previous research, which tried to just tune the original MarianMT into mentioned domains using a small portion of data gathered for a low-resource language. New architecture outperformed all previous models and gave the ability to change translation by shifting the semantic embedding.

Further tests and experiments proved that the new model indeed allows us to change the style, certain words, and structure of the translation. We showed a few examples of how our solution works for different texts and styles. Also, the way to scale this model to support more styles without any significant fine-tuning was described. Our proposed model should just get enough examples of different desired styles in the original language without any translations to capture their features and try to transfer them to the translation. We want to increase the training dataset to improve our model performance as a further development. Also, we have another idea on how to modify the embedding vector to shift it closer to the necessary state. In theory, we could build a hyperplane from the original text embedding vector and target state vectors. Then this original text can be moved by this hyperplane to affect model output.

Limitations

The most significant limitation of our research is that we did not find a way to fully interpret obtained semantic and stylistic embeddings of texts. This would allow us to make the domain change algorithm easier and more conscious. We would change just some single features or areas of the embedding vector to provide some new characteristics, which we want to see in the output. There is still a plan to get more clear interpretations to improve developed algorithms. Another limitation is related to the lack of computing resources as we could pass more data, but that would take much more time on our configuration.

Ethics Statement

The team of authors supports and agrees with the accepted ethical rules, which, in our opinion, contribute to the development of scientific activity. Such principles increase communication between authors, significantly improving the quality of the results.

References

Satanjeev Banerjee and Alon Lavie. 2005. METEOR: An automatic metric for MT evaluation with improved correlation with human judgments. In *Proceedings of the ACL Workshop on Intrinsic and Extrinsic Evaluation Measures for Machine Translation and/or Summarization*, pages 65–72, Ann Arbor, Michigan. Association for Computational Linguistics.

Tom B. Brown, Benjamin Mann, Nick Ryder, Melanie Subbiah, Jared Kaplan, Prafulla Dhariwal, Arvind Neelakantan, Pranav Shyam, Girish Sastry, Amanda Askell, Sandhini Agarwal, Ariel Herbert-Voss, Gretchen Krueger, Tom Henighan, Rewon Child, Aditya Ramesh, Daniel M. Ziegler, Jeffrey Wu,

Clemens Winter, Christopher Hesse, Mark Chen, Eric Sigler, Mateusz Litwin, Scott Gray, Benjamin Chess, Jack Clark, Christopher Berner, Sam McCandlish, Alec Radford, Ilya Sutskever, and Dario Amodei. 2020. Language models are few-shot learners. In *Proceedings of the 34th International Conference on Neural Information Processing Systems*, NIPS'20, Red Hook, NY, USA. Curran Associates Inc.

Vladimir Eidelman, Jordan Boyd-Graber, and Philip Resnik. 2012. Topic models for dynamic translation model adaptation. In *Proceedings of the 50th Annual Meeting of the Association for Computational Linguistics (Volume 2: Short Papers)*, pages 115–119, Jeju Island, Korea. Association for Computational Linguistics.

Desmond Elliott, Stella Frank, Khalil Sima'an, and Lucia Specia. 2016. Multi30K: Multilingual English-German image descriptions. In *Proceedings of the 5th Workshop on Vision and Language*, pages 70–74, Berlin, Germany. Association for Computational Linguistics.

Ye Jia, Yu Zhang, Ron J. Weiss, Quan Wang, Jonathan Shen, Fei Ren, Zhifeng Chen, Patrick Nguyen, Ruoming Pang, Ignacio Lopez Moreno, and Yonghui Wu. 2018. Transfer learning from speaker verification to multispeaker text-to-speech synthesis. In *Proceedings of the 32nd International Conference on Neural Information Processing Systems*, NIPS'18, page 4485–4495, Red Hook, NY, USA. Curran Associates Inc.

Marcin Junczys-Dowmunt, Roman Grundkiewicz, Tomasz Dwojak, Hieu Hoang, Kenneth Heafield, Tom Neckermann, Frank Seide, Ulrich Germann, Alham Fikri Aji, Nikolay Bogoychev, André F. T. Martins, and Alexandra Birch. 2018. Marian: Fast neural machine translation in C++. In *Proceedings of ACL 2018, System Demonstrations*, pages 116–121, Melbourne, Australia. Association for Computational Linguistics.

Tom Kocmi. 2020. Exploring benefits of transfer learning in neural machine translation.

Mike Lewis, Yinhan Liu, Naman Goyal, Marjan Ghazvininejad, Abdelrahman Mohamed, Omer Levy, Veselin Stoyanov, and Luke Zettlemoyer. 2020. BART: Denoising sequence-to-sequence pre-training for natural language generation, translation, and comprehension. In *Proceedings of the 58th Annual Meeting of the Association for Computational Linguistics*, pages 7871–7880, Online. Association for Computational Linguistics.

Daniil Maksymenko, Nataliia Saichyshyna, Oleksii Turuta, Olena Turuta, Andriy Yerokhin, and Andrii Babii. 2022. Improving the machine translation model in specific domains for the ukrainian language. In *2022 IEEE 17th International Conference on Computer Sciences and Information Technologies (CSIT)*, pages 123–129.

Dmytro Panchenko, Daniil Maksymenko, Olena Turuta, Mykyta Luzan, Stepan Tytarenko, and Oleksii Turuta. 2022. Ukrainian news corpus as text classification benchmark. In *ICTERI 2021 Workshops*, pages 550–559, Cham. Springer International Publishing.

Kishore Papineni, Salim Roukos, Todd Ward, and Wei-Jing Zhu. 2002. Bleu: a method for automatic evaluation of machine translation. In *Proceedings of the 40th Annual Meeting of the Association for Computational Linguistics*, pages 311–318, Philadelphia, Pennsylvania, USA. Association for Computational Linguistics.

Colin Raffel, Noam Shazeer, Adam Roberts, Katherine Lee, Sharan Narang, Michael Matena, Yanqi Zhou, Wei Li, and Peter J. Liu. 2022. Exploring the limits of transfer learning with a unified text-to-text transformer. *J. Mach. Learn. Res.*, 21(1).

Nils Reimers and Iryna Gurevych. 2019. Sentence-BERT: Sentence embeddings using Siamese BERT-networks. In *Proceedings of the 2019 Conference on Empirical Methods in Natural Language Processing and the 9th International Joint Conference on Natural Language Processing (EMNLP-IJCNLP)*, pages 3982–3992, Hong Kong, China. Association for Computational Linguistics.

Ilya Sutskever, Oriol Vinyals, and Quoc V. Le. 2014. Sequence to sequence learning with neural networks. In *Proceedings of the 27th International Conference on Neural Information Processing Systems - Volume 2*, NIPS'14, page 3104–3112, Cambridge, MA, USA. MIT Press.

Jörg Tiedemann and Santhosh Thottingal. 2020. OPUS-MT – building open translation services for the world. In *Proceedings of the 22nd Annual Conference of the European Association for Machine Translation*, pages 479–480, Lisboa, Portugal. European Association for Machine Translation.

Yongqin Xian, H. Christoph Lampert, Bernt Schiele, and Zeynep Akata. 2018. Zero-shot learning - a comprehensive evaluation of the good, the bad and the ugly. *TPAMI*.

Biao Zhang, Philip Williams, Ivan Titov, and Rico Sennrich. 2020a. Improving massively multilingual neural machine translation and zero-shot translation. In *Proceedings of the 58th Annual Meeting of the Association for Computational Linguistics*, pages 1628–1639, Online. Association for Computational Linguistics.

Tianyi Zhang, Varsha Kishore, Felix Wu, Kilian Q. Weinberger, and Yoav Artzi. 2020b. Bertscore: Evaluating text generation with BERT. In *8th International Conference on Learning Representations, ICLR 2020, Addis Ababa, Ethiopia, April 26-30, 2020*. OpenReview.net.

RooAd: A Computationally Creative Online Advertisement Generator

Mika Hämäläinen and Khalid Alnajjar
Rootroo Ltd
Helsinki, Finland
firstname@rootroo.com

Abstract

Automated generation of textual advertisements for specific products is a natural language generation problem that has not received too wide a research interest in the past. In this paper, we present a genetic algorithm based approach that models the key components of advertising: *creativity*, *ability to draw attention*, *memorability*, *clarity*, *informativeness* and *distinctiveness*. Our results suggest that our method outperforms the current state of the art in *readability* and *informativeness* but not in *attractiveness*.

1 Introduction

Generation of a variety of different kinds of creative text has received quite a lot of attention in the past years ranging from story generation (Concepción et al., 2016; Fan et al., 2018) to poem generation (Loller-Andersen and Gambäck, 2018; Hämäläinen and Alnajjar, 2019a) and humor generation (Weller et al., 2020; Alnajjar and Hämäläinen, 2021). However, one task of creative text generation that has eluded an extensive research is advertisement generation.

Advertisements need to be appealing, informative, catchy and novel. Novelty is a trait that is very important in advertising as reusing another company's advertisement for your product might in fact work in the favor of the competing company. As we will see in the related work section, the few existing approaches to advertisement generation fail to take the novelty into account.

We present a genetic algorithm based approach for computationally creative advertisement generation. We focus on short textual advertisements for products as our advertisement generator is designed to be a part of a larger online product recommendation system. For a given product recommendation, our method generates a short advertisement message.

We model our system in such a fashion that it aims to maximize the features commonly associated with computational creativity in its output. These features are *novelty*, *value* and *typicality* as identified by (Ritchie, 2007). Another way of defining computational creativity is a creative tripod framework by (Colton, 2008). According to this view, a creative system should exhibit *skill*, *imagination* and *appreciation*.

While there is a clear overlap between novelty and imagination in the two definitions, the creative tripod brings an interesting point of view to how value should be modeled. For appreciation refers to the computational system's own capacity of estimating how good or valuable its own output is based on several different parameters. Therefore, for our system it is not enough that people can see value in its output, but the system itself should also be able to evaluate its own output. The notion of typicality can be contrasted to the notion of skill; a system that has the skill of generating advertisements, must make the advertisements typical enough for them to be recognized as such.

2 Related Work

A very early approach to advertisement generation was presented by (Somers et al., 1997). They generated e-mail ads for open job positions by using a schema based approach. They store information related to the job position offered in a rule-based schema. Their system takes in ads written by people and parses them into a schema that is stored into a job ad database. When a user is looking for a job in the system, their system generate job ads based on the database and a set of grammar rules and templates. The authors do not present any evaluation of their approach.

A more recent approach that is slightly related to ad generation, is the generation of advertising plots based on a human-conducted analysis of ad videos (Ono et al., 2019). Rather than doing direct advertisement generation, the authors approach the problem from the point of view of narrative generation as the goal of their system is to generate plots for ad videos. The narratives are generated by using three principal building blocks: events, their relations and the state of the narrative.

The most recent work on advertisement generation uses two neural networks for the task; one is used for generation and the other for selection (Chan et al., 2020). They use a multi-agent communication framework in the generative neural network. They present a human evaluation of their approach, which we will use to also evaluate our system.

3 Data

Given the scarceness of publicly available ad corpora, we construct a our corpus by downloading good example ads crafted by well-known brands on social media platforms (such as Facebook, Twitter and Instagram) from AdEspresso's Academy[1]. AdEspresso provides such ads as an inspiration for beginner advertisers; however, the ads are provided as screenshots in a PDF format. To tackle this issue, we manually transcribed the textual descriptions in them. In total, the corpus contains around 1400 ad descriptions.

Following the work described by (Alnajjar and Toivonen, 2020), we build a repository of ad skeletons where ad descriptions are syntactically-parsed using spaCy (Honnibal and Montani, 2017) and, then, any content words are replaced with a placeholder. Skeletons act as an initial block for the method to build on by filling and continuously altering placeholders with words while satisfying grammatical constraints defined by the syntactical relations and optimizing multiple criteria.

We utilize a dataset of 12 million English grammatical relations (Alnajjar, 2018). A grammatical relation consists of a token, its head-token, the parts-of-speech of both tokens and the type of relation such as *nsubj* and *advmod*. In the following section we describe how these resources are harnessed in our approach.

[1] https://adespresso.com/

4 Generating Ads

In this section, we describe our genetic algorithm based approach for advertisement generation. Before doing so, it is important to define what the meaningful attributes are for advertising in general.

(Dahl, 2011) identifies six important attributes for advertisements: *creativity* (novelty), *ability to draw attention*, *memorability*, *clarity*, *informativeness* and *distinctiveness*. These are the features that we model computationally in our generative system. For the sake of simplicity, we treat creativity and distinctiveness as one attribute as they are near synonyms; both are referring to a degree of novelty in an ad. These are related to the computational creativity notions of novelty and imagination.

The remaining of the attributes are assimilated with the notions of appreciation and value in computational creativity. It is therefore important that the system is capable of assessing them individually instead of producing a single confidence score representing all of them.

The skeletons extracted in the previous section contribute to the typicality and skill of the system. When the generated ads follow an ad-like pattern and are grammatical, they are perceived more easily as ads. It is important that the output remains very ad-like as a familiar structure will make the generated ads be perceived more positively by the audience (c.f. (Veale, 2016)).

4.1 Genetic Algorithm

We opt for a genetic algorithm approach following the implementation presented in (Alnajjar et al., 2018; Alnajjar and Hämäläinen, 2018) on the DEAP tool (Fortin et al., 2012). Our implementation of the genetic algorithm takes in a random ad skeleton from the ad skeleton corpus and uses it to produce an initial population of 100 individuals. These individuals produce an offspring of another 100 individuals that go through mutation and crossover as a part of the genetic process. At the end of each generation, the individuals (ads) are scored according to the fitness functions defined

	Readability	Informativeness	Attractiveness	Rationality
Our approach	**3.672**	**3.528**	3.411	**3.373**
Chan et al., 2020	3.645	3.395	**3.500**	-

Table 1: Averages of the human evaluations in comparison with the current state-of-the-art

later in the following subsection. The 100 fittest individuals are selected with NSGA-II algorithm (Deb et al., 2002) to survive to the next generation. The individuals are picked both from the offspring and the current population so that the quality of the generated ads cannot degrade from one generation to another. This process is done for 200 generations.

All individuals in the initial population are based on a randomly selected ad and the name, description and category of the product to be advertised. We populate each ad skeleton in the initial population once by retrieving, from the grammatical relations dataset, candidate substitutions that comply with the syntactical rules imposed by the ad description. The filling process starts with the *ROOT* relation in the skeleton and continues until all placeholders are replaced with content words. Additionally, proper nouns in the skeleton are replaced by the product name that is to be advertised. This process is applied to each individual in the population, resulting in different variations of ads for the same skeleton.

In the mutation step, a random content word is picked in the ad and it is replaced by a word related to the input product in terms of the category or the description, while ensuring that the grammaticality of the expression is intact by validating that the introduced change appears in the grammatical relations dataset at least 10 times.

In terms of the crossover, we employ a single-point crossover on a word-level where one point in both individuals is selected at random and word to the right of that point are swapped.

4.2 Fitness Functions as an Internal Metric of Value

As the genetic algorithm is in the process of execution, it has to have a way of ranking its advertisements so that it can move the fittest ones to the next population and discard the worst ones. Our system uses the following five methods to rank the individual attributes of advertisements as identified by (Dahl, 2011).

4.2.1 Creativity/Distinctiveness

Novelty is an important factor in advertising, and in creative text generation, it is a parameter that is often overlooked. The degree to which a machine learning model just reproduces its training data is hardly ever discussed in any contemporary creative text generation approach (c.f. (Hämäläinen, 2020)).

In order to maximize novelty, we compare a given ad to all the ads in our ad corpus. We do this by counting BLEU scores (Papineni et al., 2002) that indicate how similar a generated ad is to an existing one. This fitness function outputs the highest BLEU score with an existing ad, and our genetic algorithm tires to minimize this parameter.

4.2.2 Ability to draw attention

We see ads all the time, but a successful one requires us to pay attention to itself, for attention is what turns what is merely seen into something that is perceived by our conscious mind (c.f (Wolfe et al., 2006)). Our brains process our surroundings by forming hypotheses and focusing less on things that follow those hypotheses and more on things that do not quite fit in. In fact, it has been argued for a long time that there is a link between surprise and attention (Horstmann, 2015). When we see something surprising, our attention is more likely to be drawn towards the surprising element.

For measuring surprise (Bunescu and Uduehi, 2019) propose using a language model (named audience model) that is separate from the model (called composer model) that is used to generate text. With the same idea, we use an AWD LSTM based language model (Merity et al., 2018) trained on another corpus to measure surprise. The less probable a sentence is according to the model, the more surprising it is. This fitness function outputs the average probability of the sentences in the ad. The genetic algorithm minimizes this value.

4.2.3 Memorability

There are several ways of improving recall in the form of applying mnemonics. The most common way for advertisements of achieving this is ensuring catchiness in the message. One way of making a message catchy is by introducing rhyme.

Rhyming is also a method for increasing memorability (c.f. (Lindstromberg and Boers, 2008)).

This fitness function counts the number of words that have rhyming pairs in the ad and divides it by the number of words, in other words it returns the proportion of words that at least rhyme with one other word in the ad. We consider several different types of rhyme: consonance, assonance, alliteration and full rhyme. We model this with simple rules. Because in English it is difficult to know how well words rhyme together based on their written form, we use Espeak-ng[2] to produce IPA transcription for each word similarly to (Hämäläinen and Alnajjar, 2019b). As IPA is supposed to relatively closely model how words are pronounced, it makes it possible to detect rhyming more accurately. The genetic algorithm tries to maximize this fitness function.

4.2.4 Clarity

For clarity, we use a previously established metric for estimating how readable texts written in English are. Flesch Reading Ease is a metric that takes into account the number of words per sentence and the number of syllables per words, with the idea that longer words and sentences result in less readable text. The higher the score, the more readable the text is. We calculate the score for each ad and our genetic algorithm tries to maximize this fitness function.

4.2.5 Informativeness

An informative ad communicates effectively information about the product. In order to ensure the ad describes the product as well as possible, we compare the meaning of the content words to the keywords of the product from its description. The comparison is done by calculating the semantic similarity of each content word in the ad with each one of the keywords by using the English FastText model by (Grave et al., 2018). The maximum similarity is picked for each word and the fitness function returns their average as a result. The genetic algorithm maximizes this value.

5 Results and Evaluation

For evaluation, we follow the evaluation approach established by (Chan et al., 2020). They evaluated their state-of-the-art approach by producing 200 ads with their system and having 3 human evaluators go through them. The evaluators were asked to rate the ads based on *readability*, *informativeness*, *attractiveness* and *rationality* on a scale from 1 to 4 (from bad to good).

We replicate their evaluation method in order to able to make a comparison to the current state-of-the-art possible. Similarly to them, we use our system to produce 200 ads for different tech products (each ad is for a different product). We present the product together with its corresponding randomly sampled ad to 3 evaluators. The first three evaluation questions are the same[3] as the previous work: *Is the ad grammatically formed and smooth?* (readability), *Does the ad contain informative words*? (informativeness), *How attractive is the ad?* (attractiveness) and *Is the ad suitable for the product?* (rationality). The last evaluation question is different for us as our system does not do product recommendation[4].

The results of the evaluation can be seen in Table 1. Our approach outperforms the current state-of-the-art in readability and informativeness, but is worse on attractiveness. The results also suggest that our method is capable of producing ads that are suitable for the product being advertised.

Are you a gamer? Nintendo Switch gives
you all the great games, experiences
and skills you want. Enhance your
gaming into the extreme
with Nintendo Switch

Above is an example of an ad produced by the system for Nintendo Switch. The advertising messages the system produces are designed to be shown in an online store for products recommended by an external system.

6 Conclusions

We have proposed a new method for generating advertisements automatically. Our method can outperform the state-of-the-art in two out of three common evaluation metrics.

We have taken an approach that is based on the main important notions of advertisements, each of which has been modeled independently as a part of the genetic algorithm. These notions, how they have been implemented in the system and their relation with computational creativity has been discussed extensively.

[2]https://github.com/espeak-ng/espeak-ng

[3]The only difference is that we use the word *ad* instead of *copywriting*

[4]The previously used question was *Is the product selection reasonable?*

Our method achieves novelty in ads as it is not trained on any existing advertisements and it continuously minimizes the similarity of its output with existing ads. At the same time it exhibits what is required by the notion of appreciation as it has several methods for assessing its own output.

References

Alnajjar, Khalid and Mika Hämäläinen. 2018. A master-apprentice approach to automatic creation of culturally satirical movie titles. In *Proceedings of the 11th International Conference on Natural Language Generation*, pages 274–283.

Alnajjar, Khalid and Mika Hämäläinen. 2021. When a computer cracks a joke: Automated generation of humorous headlines. In *Proceedings of the 12th International Conference on Computational Creativity (ICCC 2021)*. Association for Computational Creativity.

Alnajjar, Khalid and Hannu Toivonen. 2020. Computational generation of slogans. *Natural Language Engineering*, page 1–33.

Alnajjar, Khalid, Hadaytullah Hadaytullah, and Hannu Toivonen. 2018. "Talent, Skill and Support." A method for automatic creation of slogans. In *Proceedings of the 9th ICCC*, pages 88–95.

Alnajjar, Khalid. 2018. The 12 million most frequent English grammatical relations and their frequencies. https://doi.org/10.5281/zenodo.1255800, May.

Bunescu, Razvan C and Oseremen O Uduehi. 2019. Learning to surprise: A composer-audience architecture. In *ICCC*, pages 41–48.

Chan, Zhangming, Yuchi Zhang, Xiuying Chen, Shen Gao, Zhiqiang Zhang, Dongyan Zhao, and Rui Yan. 2020. Selection and generation: Learning towards multi-product advertisement post generation. In *Proceedings of EMNLP*, pages 3818–3829.

Colton, Simon. 2008. Creativity versus the perception of creativity in computational systems. In *AAAI spring symposium: creative intelligent systems*, volume 8.

Concepción, Eugenio, Pablo Gervás, and Gonzalo Méndez. 2016. Mining knowledge in storytelling systems for narrative generation. In *Proceedings of the INLG 2016 Workshop on Computational Creativity in Natural Language Generation*, pages 41–50.

Dahl, Gary. 2011. *Advertising for dummies*. John Wiley & Sons, Hoboken, New Jersey, United States.

Deb, K., A. Pratap, S. Agarwal, and T. Meyarivan. 2002. A fast and elitist multiobjective genetic algorithm: Nsga-ii. *Trans. Evol. Comp*, 6(2):182–197, April.

Fan, Angela, Mike Lewis, and Yann Dauphin. 2018. Hierarchical neural story generation. In *Proceedings of the 56th ACL (Volume 1: Long Papers)*, pages 889–898, July.

Fortin, Félix-Antoine, François-Michel De Rainville, Marc-André Gardner, Marc Parizeau, and Christian Gagné. 2012. DEAP: Evolutionary algorithms made easy. *Journal of Machine Learning Research*, 13:2171–2175, jul.

Grave, Edouard, Piotr Bojanowski, Prakhar Gupta, Armand Joulin, and Tomas Mikolov. 2018. Learning word vectors for 157 languages. In *Proceedings of LREC 2018*.

Hämäläinen, Mika and Khalid Alnajjar. 2019a. Generating modern poetry automatically in finnish. In *Proceedings of EMNLP-IJCNLP*, pages 6001–6006.

Hämäläinen, Mika and Khalid Alnajjar. 2019b. Modelling the socialization of creative agents in a master-apprentice setting: The case of movie title puns. In *Proceedings of the 10th International Conference on Computational Creativity*. Association for Computational Creativity.

Hämäläinen, Mika. 2020. *Generating Creative Language-Theories, Practice and Evaluation*. University of Helsinki.

Honnibal, Matthew and Ines Montani. 2017. spaCy 2: Natural language understanding with bloom embeddings, convolutional neural networks and incremental parsing. To appear.

Horstmann, Gernot. 2015. The surprise-attention link: a review. *Annals of the New York Academy of Sciences*, 1339(1):106–115.

Lindstromberg, Seth and Frank Boers. 2008. The Mnemonic Effect of Noticing Alliteration in Lexical Chunks. *Applied Linguistics*, 29(2):200–222, 06.

Loller-Andersen, Malte and Björn Gambäck. 2018. Deep learning-based poetry generation given visual input. In *ICCC*, pages 240–247.

Merity, Stephen, Nitish Shirish Keskar, and Richard Socher. 2018. Regularizing and optimizing lstm language models. In *International Conference on Learning Representations*.

Ono, Juumpei, Atsushi Sasaki, and Takashi Ogata. 2019. Advertising plot generation system based on comprehensive narrative analysis of advertisement videos. In *Proceedings of the 4th Workshop on Computational Creativity in Language Generation*, pages 39–46.

Papineni, Kishore, Salim Roukos, Todd Ward, and Wei-Jing Zhu. 2002. BLEU: a method for automatic evaluation of machine translation. In *Proceedings of the 40th ACL*, pages 311–318.

Ritchie, Graeme. 2007. Some empirical criteria for attributing creativity to a computer program. *Minds and Machines*, 17(1):67–99.

Somers, Harold, Bill Black, Joakim Nivre, Torbjörn Lager, Annarosa Multari, Luca Gilardoni, Jeremy Ellman, and Alex Rogers. 1997. Multilingual generation and summarization of job adverts: the tree project. In *Fifth Conference on Applied Natural Language Processing*, pages 269–276.

Veale, Tony. 2016. The shape of tweets to come: automating language play in social networks. *Multiple Perspectives on Language Play. Mouton De Gruyter, Language Play and Creativity series*, pages 73–92.

Weller, Orion, Nancy Fulda, and Kevin Seppi. 2020. Can humor prediction datasets be used for humor generation? humorous headline generation via style transfer. In *Proceedings of the Second Workshop on Figurative Language Processing*, pages 186–191.

Wolfe, Jeremy M, Keith R Kluender, Dennis M Levi, Linda M Bartoshuk, Rachel S Herz, Roberta L Klatzky, Susan J Lederman, and DM Merfeld. 2006. *Sensation & perception.* Sinauer Sunderland, MA.

Variable-length Neural Interlingua Representations for Zero-shot Neural Machine Translation

Zhuoyuan Mao [1] **Haiyue Song** [1] **Raj Dabre** [2] **Chenhui Chu** [1] **Sadao Kurohashi** [1,3]
[1] Kyoto University, Japan [2] NICT, Japan [3] NII, Japan
{zhuoyuanmao, song, chu, kuro}@nlp.ist.i.kyoto-u.ac.jp
raj.dabre@nict.go.jp

Abstract

The language-independency of encoded representations within multilingual neural machine translation (MNMT) models is crucial for their generalization ability on zero-shot translation. Neural interlingua representations have been shown as an effective method for achieving this. However, fixed-length neural interlingua representations introduced in previous work can limit its flexibility and representation ability. In this study, we introduce a novel method to enhance neural interlingua representations by making their length variable, thereby overcoming the constraint of fixed-length neural interlingua representations. Our empirical results on zero-shot translation on OPUS, IWSLT, and Europarl datasets demonstrate stable model convergence and superior zero-shot translation results compared to fixed-length neural interlingua representations. However, our analysis reveals the suboptimal efficacy of our approach in translating from certain source languages, wherein we pinpoint the defective model component in our proposed method.

1 Introduction

Multilingual neural machine translation (MNMT) (Dong et al., 2015; Firat et al., 2016; Ha et al., 2016; Johnson et al., 2017; Dabre et al., 2021) systems enable translation between multiple language pairs within a single model by learning shared representations across different languages. One of the key challenges in building effective MNMT systems is zero-shot translation performance involving unseen language pairs.

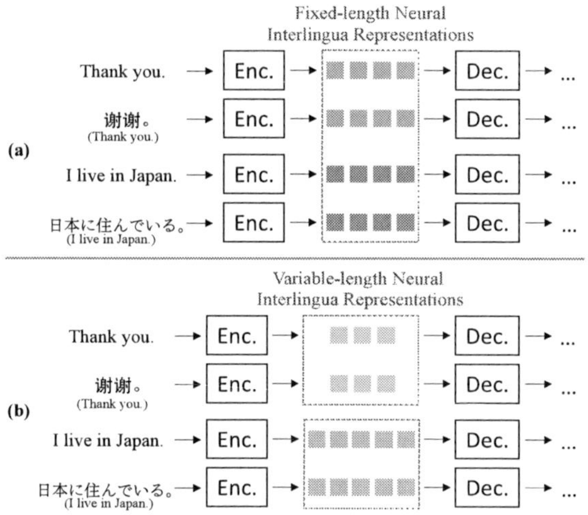

Figure 1: (a) Previous fixed-length neural interlingua representations; (b) Our proposed variable-length neural interlingua representations. Each colored box denotes the representation ($\mathbb{R}^{d\times 1}$) on the corresponding position. "Enc.", "Dec.", and "d" are encoder, decoder, and dimension of model hidden states.

Previous work reveals that improving the language-independency of encoded representations is critical for zero-shot translation performance, with neural interlingua representations (Lu et al., 2018; Vázquez et al., 2019; Zhu et al., 2020) being proposed as an effective method for achieving this. Neural interlingua representations are shared, language-independent representations that behave as a neural pivot between different natural languages. As shown in Figure 1 (a), it enables sentences in different languages with the same meaning to have the same interlingua representations. Previous work has shown the effectiveness of fixed-length neural interlingua representations for zero-shot translation. However, a fixed length can limit neural interlingua representations' flexibility and representation ability. It is highly model size and training data size-sensitive according to our experimental results for different settings of model and training data size.

This paper proposes a novel method for improving neural interlingua representations by making their length variable. As shown in Figure 1 (b), our method enables the length of the interlingua representations to vary according to different lengths of source sentences, which may provide more flexible neural interlingua representations. Specifically, we utilize the sentence length in the centric language[1] (e.g., English) as the length of neural interlingua representations. We propose a variable-length interlingua module to project sentences in different source languages with the same meaning into an identical neural interlingua representation sequence. To enable translating from non-centric language source sentences during inference, we also introduce a length predictor within the variable-length interlingua module. Moreover, as for the initialization of the interlingua module, we propose a novel method that facilitates knowledge sharing between different interlingua lengths, which can avoid introducing redundant model parameters. We expect that variable-length interlingua representations provide enhanced representations according to different source sentence lengths, which mitigates the model size and training data size-sensitive problem of previous work in low-resource scenarios and improves performance for zero-shot translation.

We conduct experiments on three MNMT datasets, OPUS (Zhang et al., 2020), IWSLT (Cettolo et al., 2017), and Europarl (Koehn, 2005) with different settings of training data size and model size. Results demonstrate that our proposed method yields superior results for zero-shot translation compared to previous work. Our method exhibits stable convergence in different settings while previous work (Zhu et al., 2020) is highly sensitive to different model and training data sizes. However, we also observe the inferior performance of our method for translation from non-centric language source languages. We attribute it to the accuracy of the interlingua length predictor and point out the possible directions of this research line.

[1]In this work, we consider using an x-centric parallel corpus, wherein all sentence pairs within the corpus consist of sentences in language x paired with another language. It is noteworthy that the English-centric corpus is the most prevalent setting. We denote a language distinct from x as a "non-centric language" in the subsequent text.

2 Related Work

This paper focuses on variable-length interlingua representations for zero-shot NMT.

2.1 Zero-shot Translation

In recent years, MNMT (Dong et al., 2015; Firat et al., 2016; Ha et al., 2016; Johnson et al., 2017; Aharoni et al., 2019; Tan et al., 2019; Dabre et al., 2021; Zhang et al., 2020) has been a popular research topic, where the generalization ability of MNMT models to zero-shot translation is a critical problem as obtaining sufficient training data for all translation directions is often impractical. An MNMT model's zero-shot translation performance usually benefits from the encoder-side representations being language-independent and decoder-side representations being language-specific. To achieve this, some studies have proposed removing encoder-side residual connections (Liu et al., 2021) or introducing language-independent constraints (Al-Shedivat and Parikh, 2019; Pham et al., 2019; Arivazhagan et al., 2019; Yang et al., 2021; Mao et al., 2023). Other methods involve decoder pre-training and back-translation (Gu et al., 2019; Zhang et al., 2020), denoising autoencoder objectives (Wang et al., 2021), and encoder-side neural interlingua representations (Lu et al., 2018; Vázquez et al., 2019; Zhu et al., 2020).

2.2 Neural Interlingua Representations for Zero-shot Translation

As mentioned above, constructing neural interlingua representations is a powerful method to improve shared encoder representations across various source languages and enhance zero-shot translation. Lu et al. (2018) first proposed the concept of neural interlingua representations for MNMT, intending to bridge multiple language-specific encoders and decoders using an intermediate interlingua attention module, which has a fixed sequence length. Vázquez et al. (2019) extended this approach with a universal encoder and decoder architecture for MNMT and introduced a regularization objective for the interlingua attention similarity matrix. More recently, Zhu et al. (2020) applied the neural interlingua approach in the Trans-

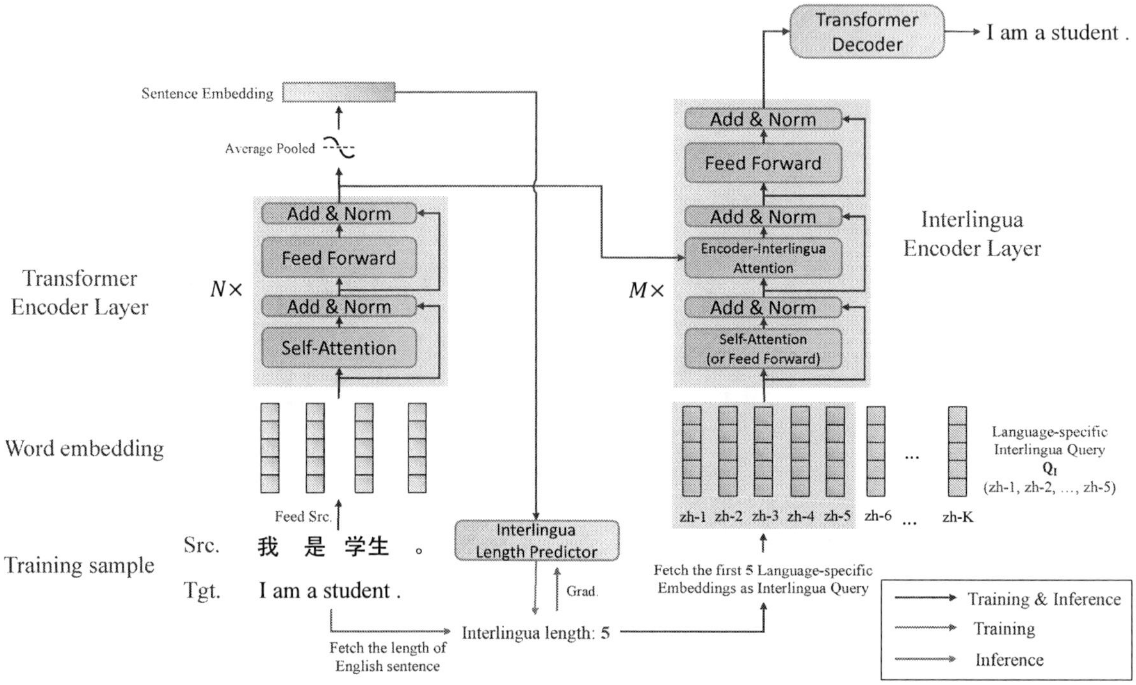

Figure 2: Variable-length interlingua module. "zh-x" denotes the x-th embedding of a Chinese-specific interlingua query.

former (Vaswani et al., 2017) model architecture and proposed a position-wise alignment objective to ensure consistent neural interlingua representations across different languages. However, these methods utilized fixed-length neural interlingua representations, which may reduce the model's representation ability for source sentences with different lengths. This paper focuses on revisiting and improving neural interlingua approaches.

3 Variable-length Neural Interlingua Representations

We present an MNMT model that comprises three distinct components: a source language encoder, a neural interlingua module, and a decoder. The source language encoder converts source sentences to language-specific representations, the neural interlingua module generates language-agnostic representations, and the decoder converts these representations into the target language translation. In this section, we introduce a novel neural interlingua module.

Specifically, we propose variable-length neural interlingua representations surpassing prior work's fixed-length constraint. To achieve this breakthrough, we have developed a module that includes interlingua encoder layers, an interlingua length predictor, and a language-specific interlingua query. Our module uses an embedding sharing mechanism, as shown in Figure 2. Moreover, we introduce the objectives that guide the training of variable-length neural interlingua representations.

3.1 Variable-length Interlingua Module

Interlingua Encoder Layers In accordance with Zhu et al. (2020), we construct a variable-length interlingua module within a Transformer model architecture. Our model utilizes N Transformer encoder layers and 6 Transformer decoder layers, with M interlingua encoder layers introduced between them. To maintain consistency with a standard 6-layer Transformer encoder, we set $M + N = 6$, ensuring that the number of model parameters remains almost the same. Each interlingua encoder layer consists of a sequential series of operations, including self-attention mechanisms (or feed-forward networks),[2] encoder-interlingua attention, and feed-forward networks, as illustrated in Figure 2.

The input representations for interlingua encoder layers are denoted as $\mathbf{Q}_\mathrm{I} \in \mathbb{R}^{d \times \mathrm{len}_\mathrm{I}(X)}$, where d and $\mathrm{len}_\mathrm{I}(X)$ respectively indicates the di-

[2]We utilize feed-forward networks for the first interlingua encoder layer and employ a self-attention mechanism for subsequent layers. This is because the interlingua query is initially weak and unable to capture similarities through a self-attention mechanism. This design choice is similar to that of Zhu et al. (2020).

mension of hidden representations and the length of the neural interlingua representations given a source sentence $X = x_1, x_2, ..., x_k$. Specifically, we define $\text{len}_\text{I}(X)$ as follows:

$$\text{len}_\text{I}(X) = \begin{cases} \text{len}(X), & X \text{is in centric} \\ \text{len}(\text{CT}(X)), & X \text{is in non-centric} \end{cases}, \quad (1)$$

where $\text{CT}(X)$ denotes the translation of X in the centric language. We use teacher forcing to generate interlingua length during training. For instance, if we use English-centric parallel sentences as training data, $\text{len}_\text{I}(X)$ for each sentence pair will be the length of English sentences. Thus, sentences that convey the same semantic meaning can have the same interlingua length, and interlingua length is variable according to different sentences. For the initialization of $\mathbf{Q}_\text{I}$, we will provide a detailed explanation of how to generate it later in this section.

Subsequently, $\mathbf{Q}_\text{I}$ undergoes self-attention (or feed-forward networks), and we obtain the output $\mathbf{Q}_\text{I}^{'}$. Assume that the contextualized representations on top of N Transformer encoder layers are $\mathbf{H}_\text{S} \in \mathbb{R}^{d \times k}$. Then we establish an encoder-interlingua attention mechanism:

$$\mathbf{H}_\text{EI} = \text{Attn}(\mathbf{Q}_\text{I}^{'}, \mathbf{H}_\text{S}, \mathbf{H}_\text{S}), \quad (2)$$

where $\text{Attn}(\mathbf{Q}, \mathbf{K}, \mathbf{V})$ indicates the multi-head attention mechanism (Vaswani et al., 2017). This encoder-interlingua attention inherits the design in previous studies of neural interlingua representations (Lu et al., 2018; Vázquez et al., 2019; Zhu et al., 2020).

Finally, we pass $\mathbf{H}_\text{EI}$ through position-wise feed-forward networks to obtain $\mathbf{H}_\text{I}$, the output of the interlingua encoder layers. $\mathbf{H}_\text{I}$ serves as a language-agnostic neural interlingua and can vary in length depending on the source sentence. Once we have $\mathbf{H}_\text{I}$, we feed it into a standard Transformer decoder to generate the translation.

Interlingua Length Predictor Length of interlingua representations is not readily available during inference when translating from non-centric source sentences (e.g., non-English source sentences) using Eq. (1). To address this, we propose using an interlingua length predictor to obtain $\text{len}_\text{I}(X)$ for inference. Specifically, we treat the length prediction of translation in the centric language as a classification task, addressed utilizing mean pooled contextualized representations atop the Transformer encoder.[3] More precisely, we predict X's interlingua length as:

$$\text{len}_\text{I}(X) = \arg\max_i \text{ softmax}(\frac{\mathbf{1}\,\mathbf{H}_\text{S}^\text{T}}{k}\mathbf{W} + \mathbf{b})_i, \quad (3)$$

where k is the length of X, $\mathbf{1} \in \mathbb{R}^{1 \times k}$ denotes a vector with all the elements of 1, $\mathbf{W} \in \mathbb{R}^{d \times K}$ and $\mathbf{b} \in \mathbb{R}^{1 \times K}$ indicates the weight and bias of a linear layer, and K is the maximum sequence length allowed in the model.

Language-specific Interlingua Query Here, we present the method for obtaining input representations $\mathbf{Q}_\text{I}$ for the interlingua encoder layers. Initially, we randomly initialize an embedding matrix $\mathbf{E}_l \in \mathbb{R}^{d \times K}$ containing K embeddings for the source language l. Next, we extract the first $\text{len}_\text{I}(X)$ embeddings from $\mathbf{E}_l$ to obtain $\mathbf{Q}_\text{I}$.

$$\mathbf{Q}_\text{I} = \mathbf{E}_l \mathbf{I}_\text{S}, \quad (4)$$

where $\mathbf{I}_\text{S} \in \mathbb{R}^{K \times \text{len}_\text{I}(X)}$ has 1s as main diagonal elements and 0s for other elements. Note that the language-specific nature of $\mathbf{E}_l$ allows the model to learn a unique mapping from each language to the neural interlingua representations. Zhu et al. (2020) used the technique of language-aware positional embedding (Wang et al., 2019) for both the neural interlingua representations and the source and target sentences, resulting in ambiguity regarding whether the improvements were from the neural interlingua representations or not. In contrast, our proposed language-specific interlingua query clarifies whether a language-specific mapping to neural interlingua representations benefits zero-shot translation.

3.2 Training Objectives

Given a training sample sentence pair (X, Y), we introduce the following training objective, combining an NMT loss, an interlingua alignment loss, and a length prediction loss. The interlingua alignment loss is utilized to guarantee the consistency of the neural interlingua representations for each training sentence pair sample. In contrast, the length prediction loss ensures the generation of variable interlingua length during inference. Specifically, the training objective is defined as follows:

$$\mathcal{L}(X, Y) = \alpha\mathcal{L}_\text{NMT} + \beta\mathcal{L}_\text{IA} + \gamma\mathcal{L}_\text{LP}, \quad (5)$$

[3]We attempted to treat it as a regression task, but the performance of the regression model was notably inferior to that of the classifier-based predictor.

Datasets	Languages	# Sup.	# Zero.	# Train	# Valid	# Test
OPUS	ar, de, en, fr, nl, ru, zh	12	30	12,000,000	2,000	2,000
IWSLT	en, it, nl, ro	6	6	1,378,794	2,562	1,147
Europarl	de, en, es, fr, nl	8	12	15,782,882	2,000	2,000

Table 1: Statistics of the training data. "# Sup." and "# Zero." indicate the respective number of language pairs for supervised and zero-shot translation. "# Train" denotes the total number of the training parallel sentences while "# Valid" and "# Test" showcase the number per language pair.

where α, β, and γ are weight hyperparameters for each loss, $\mathcal{L}_{\text{LP}}$ is a cross-entropy loss computed from the softmax outputs from Eq. (3), and $\mathcal{L}_{\text{IA}}$ is a position-wise alignment loss using cosine similarity following Zhu et al. (2020):

$$\mathcal{L}_{\text{IA}} = 1 - \frac{1}{\text{len}_{\text{I}}(X)} \sum_i \cos < \mathbf{H}_{\text{I}}(X)_i, \mathbf{H}_{\text{I}}(Y)_i > . \quad (6)$$

Here $\mathbf{H}_{\text{I}}(\cdot)_i$ denotes the i-th column of $\mathbf{H}_{\text{I}}(\cdot)$.[4] Please note that during training, we always have $\text{len}_{\text{I}}(X) = \text{len}_{\text{I}}(Y)$ because we apply teacher forcing to generate the interlingua length for the sentence pair (X, Y). With $\mathcal{L}_{\text{IA}}$, different sentence pairs with varying lengths of translation in centric language can be represented using variable-length neural interlingua representations. This can enhance the bridging ability for zero-shot translation.

4 Experimental Settings

4.1 Datasets

Our study involves conducting experiments on zero-shot translation using three distinct datasets, OPUS (Zhang et al., 2020), IWSLT (Cettolo et al., 2017), and Europarl (Koehn, 2005), each comprising 7, 4, and 5 languages, respectively. For each dataset, we adopt the train, valid, and test splits following Zhang et al. (2020), Wu et al. (2021), and Liu et al. (2021). Table 1 presents each dataset's overall statistics. The training and validation data exclusively contains English-centric sentence pairs, indicating the centric language is English in all the experiments, leading to 12, 6, and 8 supervised directions, and 30, 6, and 12 zero-shot directions for each dataset. Refer to Appendix A for preprocessing details.

4.2 Overall Training and Evaluation Details

For the OPUS and IWSLT datasets, we utilize a `Transformer-base` model, while for Europarl, we employ a `Transformer-big` model, to evaluate the performance of Transformer with both sufficient and insufficient training data. Regarding language tag strategies to indicate the source and target languages to the model, we adopt the method of appending the source language tag to the encoder input and the target language tag to the decoder input (Liu et al., 2020). This approach allows for the creation of fully language-agnostic neural interlingua representations in between.[5] The maximum sentence length is set as 256, which indicates that $K = 256$ (Section 3.1). Refer to Appendix B for other training details.

For evaluation, we choose the evaluation checkpoint based on the validation $\mathcal{L}_{\text{NMT}}$ with the lowest value. We use a beam size of 5 during inference on the trained models to conduct inference. We report SacreBLEU (Post, 2018).[6]

4.3 Baselines and Respective Training Details

To compare our variable-length neural interlingua method with previous fixed-length neural interlingua methods, we trained the following settings:

MNMT (Johnson et al., 2017) is a system trained with standard `Transformer-base` or `Transformer-big` for multiple language pairs. We applied the language tag strategy of source language tag for encoder input and target language tag for decoder input.

Pivot translation (Zoph and Knight, 2016) involves translating a source language into a pivot language, usually English, and then translating the pivot language into the target language. This system constitutes a robust baseline for zero-shot translation, which we include for reference. We implement this setting by feeding the pivot language output of the MNMT model to itself to generate the target language.

Len-fix. Uni. Intl. We follow the setting described by Zhu et al. (2020), but we remove its language-aware positional embedding to test whether a single interlingua module can improve zero-shot translation. Compared to our variable-length interlingua representations presented in Section 3.1, these fixed interlingua representations have a universal len_{I} (Eq. (1)) for different source

[4]To derive $\mathbf{H}_{\text{I}}(Y)$, it is necessary to feed the target sentence to both the encoder and interlingua encoder layers, which can potentially result in increased computational requirements.

[5]We do not consider employing target language tag appending on the encoder-side (Johnson et al., 2017) in this work because it would require removing both the source and target language information after feeding the source sentence to obtain the neural interlingua representations.

[6]We utilize the "zh" tokenization mode for Chinese, and the "13a" tokenization mode for other languages.

Methods	Zero-shot			Supervised: From en			Supervised: To en		
	OPUS	IWSLT	Europarl	OPUS	IWSLT	Europarl	OPUS	IWSLT	Europarl
Pivot	*22.0*	*19.9*	*29.5*	-	-	-	-	-	-
MNMT	16.5	13.1	29.0	**31.2**	**29.6**	**32.9**	**36.8**	**33.5**	**36.1**
Len-fix. Uni. Intl.	18.2	12.7	17.4	29.6	19.6	20.1	35.3	22.2	21.8
Len-fix. LS. Intl.	18.4	4.7	5.8	30.1	7.3	6.7	35.7	12.9	7.1
Len-vari. Intl. (ours)	**18.9**†	**14.8**	**29.6**	30.2†	26.2	32.6	34.0	27.1	33.8

Table 2: Overall BLEU results on OPUS, IWSLT, and Europarl. The best result among all the settings except *Pivot* is in **bold**. We mark the results significantly (Koehn, 2004) better than "Len-fix. Uni. Intl." with † for OPUS dataset.

Methods	de–fr		ru–fr		nl–de		zh–ru		zh–ar		nl–ar		Zero-shot
	→	←	→	←	→	←	→	←	→	←	→	←	Avg.
Pivot	*23.4*	*21.2*	*31.0*	*26.0*	*21.8*	*23.6*	*24.8*	*37.9*	*24.0*	*38.9*	*7.4*	*17.4*	*22.0*
MNMT	17.6	15.0	21.5	17.7	17.9	21.4	15.3	27.6	18.0	28.6	5.3	13.3	16.5
Len-fix. Uni. Intl.	20.1	17.0	25.0	22.4	19.5	21.3	20.3	30.9	19.6	30.4	6.1	14.4	18.2
Len-fix. LS. Intl.	**20.7**	17.7	25.7	21.7	19.8	21.6	19.9	31.5	**20.1**	31.6	**6.5**	**14.5**	18.4
Len-vari. Intl. (ours)	20.6†	**18.3**†	**26.0**†	**23.4**†	**20.2**†	**22.1**†	**20.8**	**31.8**†	20.0	**31.9**†	6.3	**14.5**	**18.9**†

Table 3: BLEU results of zero-shot translation on OPUS. We randomly select six zero-shot language pairs and report the results. The best result among all the settings except "*Pivot*" is in **bold**. We mark the results significantly (Koehn, 2004) better than "Len-fix. Uni. Intl." with †.

sentences and a universal $\mathbf{E} \in \mathbb{R}^{d \times \text{len}_\text{I}}$ for different languages and without a $\mathbf{Q}_\text{I}$ (Eq. (4)). The fixed interlingua length is set to 17, 21, and 30, which are the average lengths of each dataset following Zhu et al. (2020) and Vázquez et al. (2019).

Len-fix. LS. Intl. The only difference between this system and the "Len-fix. Uni. Intl." system mentioned above is the initialization of the interlingua query. We use a language-specific $\mathbf{E}_l \in \mathbb{R}^{d \times \text{len}_\text{I}}$ for each source language l without a $\mathbf{Q}_\text{I}$ (Eq. (4)).

Len-vari. Intl. (ours) This refers to variable-length neural interlingua representations proposed in Section 3.

For the last three neural interlingua settings, we set M and N to 3 for both the Transformer encoder and interlingua encoder layers. The values of α, β, and γ (Eq. (5)) are set as 1.0, 1.0, and 0.1, respectively. We remove the first residual connection within the first interlingua encoder layer to improve the language-independency of the interlingua representations, inspired by Liu et al. (2021).

5 Results and Analysis

We now present in tables 2, 3, and 4 the results of our variable-length interlingua approach and compare them against several baselines.

5.1 Main results

Firstly, Tables 2 and 3 indicate that our proposed variable-length interlingua representations outperform previous work in zero-shot directions. The severe overfitting issue of "Len-fix. Uni. Intl." and "Len-fix. LS. Intl." on IWSLT and Europarl suggests that they are limited to model size and training data size settings, while our proposed method can converge stably on all three settings. These results demonstrate that our flexible interlingua length can benefit zero-shot translation more effectively. Secondly, our proposed method performs better than previous work in "from en" supervised directions as shown in Tables 2 and 4, but still falls short of the MNMT baseline. This may be attributed to the interlingua module's weak source-target awareness. Thirdly, our variable-length neural interlingua representations perform significantly worse on "to en" directions than "Len-fix." methods on OPUS and MNMT on all datasets. We provide analysis of this phenomenon next.

5.2 Validation NMT Loss

We investigate why variable-length neural interlingua representations perform poorly in "to en" supervised directions by analyzing the validation NMT loss, an approximate measure of NMT performance on the validation set. Figure 3 displays the validation NMT loss for all settings on OPUS. We observe that variable-length interlingua representations can converge well, even smaller than the validation loss of "Len-fix. Uni. Intl." and "Len-fix. LS. Intl." However, the interlingua length predictor was teacher-forced during training, indicat-

Methods	en–ar →	en–ar ←	en–de →	en–de ←	en–fr →	en–fr ←	en–nl →	en–nl ←	en–ru →	en–ru ←	en–zh →	en–zh ←	Supervised Avg. From en	Supervised Avg. To en
MNMT	**23.9**	**37.8**	**30.8**	**34.6**	**33.9**	**35.5**	**27.8**	**31.5**	29.4	**35.1**	**41.2**	**46.4**	**31.2**	**36.8**
Len-fix. Uni. Intl.	22.6	36.6	28.9	33.0	31.7	33.5	27.4	30.1	28.4	34.0	38.8	44.6	29.6	35.3
Len-fix. LS. Intl.	22.9	36.8	29.0	33.8	32.3	33.9	27.7	30.6	28.9	34.3	39.5	44.8	30.1	35.7
Len-vari. Intl. (ours)	23.3†	33.8	30.1†	32.3	32.9†	32.6	27.3	27.9	**29.5**†	32.2	38.0	45.3†	30.2†	34.0

Table 4: BLEU results of supervised translation on OPUS. The best result among all the settings is in **bold**. We mark the results significantly (Koehn, 2004) better than "Len-fix. Uni. Intl." with †.

	ar	de	fr	nl	ru	zh	Avg.
Acc. of Len. Pre.	20.6	26.5	17.6	19.3	21.1	13.8	19.8
Avg. of | Len. Pre. − *gold* |	2.4	3.4	3.8	3.1	3.3	3.9	3.3
BLEU w/ Len. Pre.	33.8	32.3	32.6	27.9	32.2	45.3	34.0
BLEU w/ *gold*	35.5†	33.4†	33.3†	29.4†	33.4†	46.0†	35.2†

Table 5: Accuracy of the interlingua length predictor, averaged absolute difference between predicted length and *gold* length, and "to en" BLEU scores of each non-English source language on OPUS. "w/ Len. Pre." and "w/ *gold*" indicate using the predicted interlingua length and the correct interlingua length (length of the English translation), respectively. Accuracy of the length predictor and average abosulute difference are evaluated using OPUS's test set. We mark the results significantly (Koehn, 2004) better than "BLEU w/ Len. Pre." with †.

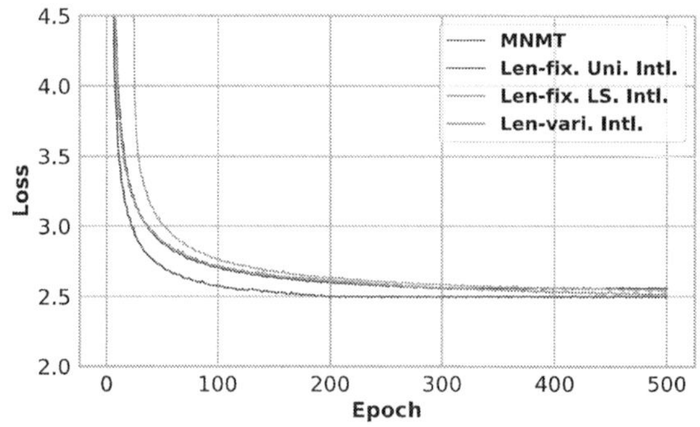

Figure 3: Validation NMT loss curve on OPUS.

ing the validation NMT loss was calculated with a 100% accurate interlingua length predictor. As a result, the inaccurate interlingua length predictor is likely the primary cause of our method's inferior performance in "to en" directions, despite its well-converged validation NMT loss.

5.3 Impact of the Interlingua Length Predictor

We analyze the interlingua length predictor and identify the reason for the subpar performance in "to en" translations. We input the source sentences of the test set in non-English languages into the model and check whether the predicted length in interlingua is identical to the length of its English reference. We present the accuracy on the OPUS dataset in Table 5. The results show that the accuracy for each language is approximately 20.0%, which can result in error propagation when translating from those languages. To further understand the impact of the length predictor quality on translation performance, we attempt to provide the model with the correct interlingua length instead of relying on the length predictor. As shown in Table 5, the results reveal significant BLEU improvements when the correct interlingua length is applied. This suggests that the performance issue encountered when translating from a non-centric source language can be addressed by upgrading the interlingua length predictor's accuracy. Furthermore, we can also enhance zero-shot translation performance if we have a better length predictor. Nevertheless, we observe that even with a low length prediction accuracy of approximately 20.0%, we can still achieve solid BLEU performance, averaging 34.0 BLEU points. This indicates that an incorrectly predicted length with just a trivial difference, as shown in Table 5, will not result in the enormous information loss required for translation.

6 Conclusion

This study introduced a novel variable-length neural interlingua approach that improved zero-shot translation results while providing a more stable model than previous fixed-length interlingua methods. Although our analysis revealed a performance downgrade in "to en" directions, we have identified the problematic model component and plan to address it in future studies.

Acknowledgements

This work was supported by JSPS KAKENHI Grant Number 22KJ1843.

References

Aharoni, Roee, Melvin Johnson, and Orhan Firat. 2019. Massively multilingual neural machine translation. In *Proceedings of the 2019 Conference of the North American Chapter of the Association for Computational Linguistics: Human Language Technologies, Volume 1 (Long and Short Papers)*, pages 3874–3884, Minneapolis, Minnesota, June. Association for Computational Linguistics.

Al-Shedivat, Maruan and Ankur Parikh. 2019. Consistency by agreement in zero-shot neural machine translation. In *Proceedings of the 2019 Conference of the North American Chapter of the Association for Computational Linguistics: Human Language Technologies, Volume 1 (Long and Short Papers)*, pages 1184–1197, Minneapolis, Minnesota, June. Association for Computational Linguistics.

Arivazhagan, Naveen, Ankur Bapna, Orhan Firat, Roee Aharoni, Melvin Johnson, and Wolfgang Macherey. 2019. The missing ingredient in zero-shot neural machine translation. *CoRR*, abs/1903.07091.

Cettolo, Mauro, Marcello Federico, Luisa Bentivogli, Jan Niehues, Sebastian Stüker, Katsuhito Sudoh, Koichiro Yoshino, and Christian Federmann. 2017. Overview of the IWSLT 2017 evaluation campaign. In *Proceedings of the 14th International Conference on Spoken Language Translation*, pages 2–14, Tokyo, Japan, December 14-15. International Workshop on Spoken Language Translation.

Dabre, Raj, Chenhui Chu, and Anoop Kunchukuttan. 2021. A survey of multilingual neural machine translation. *ACM Comput. Surv.*, 53(5):99:1–99:38.

Dong, Daxiang, Hua Wu, Wei He, Dianhai Yu, and Haifeng Wang. 2015. Multi-task learning for multiple language translation. In *Proceedings of the 53rd Annual Meeting of the Association for Computational Linguistics and the 7th International Joint Conference on Natural Language Processing (Volume 1: Long Papers)*, pages 1723–1732, Beijing, China, July. Association for Computational Linguistics.

Firat, Orhan, Kyunghyun Cho, and Yoshua Bengio. 2016. Multi-way, multilingual neural machine translation with a shared attention mechanism. In *Proceedings of the 2016 Conference of the North American Chapter of the Association for Computational Linguistics: Human Language Technologies*, pages 866–875, San Diego, California, June. Association for Computational Linguistics.

Gu, Jiatao, Yong Wang, Kyunghyun Cho, and Victor O.K. Li. 2019. Improved zero-shot neural machine translation via ignoring spurious correlations. In *Proceedings of the 57th Annual Meeting of the Association for Computational Linguistics*, pages 1258–1268, Florence, Italy, July. Association for Computational Linguistics.

Ha, Thanh-Le, Jan Niehues, and Alex Waibel. 2016. Toward multilingual neural machine translation with universal encoder and decoder. In *Proceedings of the 13th International Conference on Spoken Language Translation*, Seattle, Washington D.C, December 8-9. International Workshop on Spoken Language Translation.

Hu, Junjie, Sebastian Ruder, Aditya Siddhant, Graham Neubig, Orhan Firat, and Melvin Johnson. 2020. XTREME: A massively multilingual multitask benchmark for evaluating cross-lingual generalisation. In *Proceedings of the 37th International Conference on Machine Learning, ICML 2020, 13-18 July 2020, Virtual Event*, volume 119 of *Proceedings of Machine Learning Research*, pages 4411–4421. PMLR.

Johnson, Melvin, Mike Schuster, Quoc V. Le, Maxim Krikun, Yonghui Wu, Zhifeng Chen, Nikhil Thorat, Fernanda Viégas, Martin Wattenberg, Greg Corrado, Macduff Hughes, and Jeffrey Dean. 2017. Google's multilingual neural machine translation system: Enabling zero-shot translation. *Transactions of the Association for Computational Linguistics*, 5:339–351.

Kingma, Diederik P. and Jimmy Ba. 2015. Adam: A method for stochastic optimization. In Bengio, Yoshua and Yann LeCun, editors, *3rd International Conference on Learning Representations, ICLR 2015, San Diego, CA, USA, May 7-9, 2015, Conference Track Proceedings*.

Koehn, Philipp, Hieu Hoang, Alexandra Birch, Chris Callison-Burch, Marcello Federico, Nicola Bertoldi, Brooke Cowan, Wade Shen, Christine Moran, Richard Zens, Chris Dyer, Ondřej Bojar, Alexandra Constantin, and Evan Herbst. 2007. Moses: Open source toolkit for statistical machine translation. In *Proceedings of the 45th Annual Meeting of the Association for Computational Linguistics Companion Volume Proceedings of the Demo and Poster Sessions*, pages 177–180, Prague, Czech Republic, June. Association for Computational Linguistics.

Koehn, Philipp. 2004. Statistical significance tests for machine translation evaluation. In *Proceedings of the 2004 Conference on Empirical Methods in Natural Language Processing*, pages 388–395, Barcelona, Spain, July. Association for Computational Linguistics.

Koehn, Philipp. 2005. Europarl: A parallel corpus for statistical machine translation. In *Proceedings of Machine Translation Summit X: Papers, MTSummit 2005, Phuket, Thailand, September 13-15, 2005*, pages 79–86.

Liu, Yinhan, Jiatao Gu, Naman Goyal, Xian Li, Sergey Edunov, Marjan Ghazvininejad, Mike Lewis, and

Luke Zettlemoyer. 2020. Multilingual denoising pre-training for neural machine translation. *Transactions of the Association for Computational Linguistics*, 8:726–742.

Liu, Danni, Jan Niehues, James Cross, Francisco Guzmán, and Xian Li. 2021. Improving zero-shot translation by disentangling positional information. In *Proceedings of the 59th Annual Meeting of the Association for Computational Linguistics and the 11th International Joint Conference on Natural Language Processing (Volume 1: Long Papers)*, pages 1259–1273, Online, August. Association for Computational Linguistics.

Lu, Yichao, Phillip Keung, Faisal Ladhak, Vikas Bhardwaj, Shaonan Zhang, and Jason Sun. 2018. A neural interlingua for multilingual machine translation. In *Proceedings of the Third Conference on Machine Translation: Research Papers*, pages 84–92, Brussels, Belgium, October. Association for Computational Linguistics.

Mao, Zhuoyuan, Raj Dabre, Qianying Liu, Haiyue Song, Chenhui Chu, and Sadao Kurohashi. 2023. Exploring the impact of layer normalization for zero-shot neural machine translation. *CoRR*, abs/2305.09312.

Micikevicius, Paulius, Sharan Narang, Jonah Alben, Gregory F. Diamos, Erich Elsen, David García, Boris Ginsburg, Michael Houston, Oleksii Kuchaiev, Ganesh Venkatesh, and Hao Wu. 2018. Mixed precision training. In *6th International Conference on Learning Representations, ICLR 2018, Vancouver, BC, Canada, April 30 - May 3, 2018, Conference Track Proceedings*. OpenReview.net.

Pham, Ngoc-Quan, Jan Niehues, Thanh-Le Ha, and Alexander Waibel. 2019. Improving zero-shot translation with language-independent constraints. In *Proceedings of the Fourth Conference on Machine Translation (Volume 1: Research Papers)*, pages 13–23, Florence, Italy, August. Association for Computational Linguistics.

Post, Matt. 2018. A call for clarity in reporting BLEU scores. In *Proceedings of the Third Conference on Machine Translation: Research Papers*, pages 186–191, Brussels, Belgium, October. Association for Computational Linguistics.

Sennrich, Rico, Barry Haddow, and Alexandra Birch. 2016. Neural machine translation of rare words with subword units. In *Proceedings of the 54th Annual Meeting of the Association for Computational Linguistics (Volume 1: Long Papers)*, pages 1715–1725, Berlin, Germany, August. Association for Computational Linguistics.

Tan, Xu, Jiale Chen, Di He, Yingce Xia, Tao Qin, and Tie-Yan Liu. 2019. Multilingual neural machine translation with language clustering. In *Proceedings of the 2019 Conference on Empirical Methods in Natural Language Processing and the 9th International Joint Conference on Natural Language Processing (EMNLP-IJCNLP)*, pages 963–973, Hong Kong, China, November. Association for Computational Linguistics.

Vaswani, Ashish, Noam Shazeer, Niki Parmar, Jakob Uszkoreit, Llion Jones, Aidan N. Gomez, Lukasz Kaiser, and Illia Polosukhin. 2017. Attention is all you need. In Guyon, Isabelle, Ulrike von Luxburg, Samy Bengio, Hanna M. Wallach, Rob Fergus, S. V. N. Vishwanathan, and Roman Garnett, editors, *Advances in Neural Information Processing Systems 30: Annual Conference on Neural Information Processing Systems 2017, December 4-9, 2017, Long Beach, CA, USA*, pages 5998–6008.

Vázquez, Raúl, Alessandro Raganato, Jörg Tiedemann, and Mathias Creutz. 2019. Multilingual NMT with a language-independent attention bridge. In *Proceedings of the 4th Workshop on Representation Learning for NLP (RepL4NLP-2019)*, pages 33–39, Florence, Italy, August. Association for Computational Linguistics.

Wang, Xinyi, Hieu Pham, Philip Arthur, and Graham Neubig. 2019. Multilingual neural machine translation with soft decoupled encoding. In *7th International Conference on Learning Representations, ICLR 2019, New Orleans, LA, USA, May 6-9, 2019*. OpenReview.net.

Wang, Weizhi, Zhirui Zhang, Yichao Du, Boxing Chen, Jun Xie, and Weihua Luo. 2021. Rethinking zero-shot neural machine translation: From a perspective of latent variables. In *Findings of the Association for Computational Linguistics: EMNLP 2021*, pages 4321–4327, Punta Cana, Dominican Republic, November. Association for Computational Linguistics.

Wu, Liwei, Shanbo Cheng, Mingxuan Wang, and Lei Li. 2021. Language tags matter for zero-shot neural machine translation. In *Findings of the Association for Computational Linguistics: ACL-IJCNLP 2021*, pages 3001–3007, Online, August. Association for Computational Linguistics.

Yang, Yilin, Akiko Eriguchi, Alexandre Muzio, Prasad Tadepalli, Stefan Lee, and Hany Hassan. 2021. Improving multilingual translation by representation and gradient regularization. In *Proceedings of the 2021 Conference on Empirical Methods in Natural Language Processing*, pages 7266–7279, Online and Punta Cana, Dominican Republic, November. Association for Computational Linguistics.

Zhang, Biao, Philip Williams, Ivan Titov, and Rico Sennrich. 2020. Improving massively multilingual neural machine translation and zero-shot translation. In *Proceedings of the 58th Annual Meeting of the Association for Computational Linguistics*, pages 1628–1639, Online, July. Association for Computational Linguistics.

Zhu, Changfeng, Heng Yu, Shanbo Cheng, and Weihua Luo. 2020. Language-aware interlingua for multilingual neural machine translation. In *Proceedings of the 58th Annual Meeting of the Association for Computational Linguistics*, pages 1650–1655, Online, July. Association for Computational Linguistics.

Zoph, Barret and Kevin Knight. 2016. Multi-source neural translation. In *Proceedings of the 2016 Conference of the North American Chapter of the Association for Computational Linguistics: Human Language Technologies*, pages 30–34, San Diego, California, June. Association for Computational Linguistics.

A Preprocessing Details

Jieba[7] is used to segment Chinese while Moses[8] (Koehn et al., 2007) is utilized to tokenize other languages. We employ BPE (Sennrich et al., 2016) with $50,000$, $40,000$, and $50,000$ merge operations to create a joint vocabulary for each dataset, resulting in the vocabulary sizes of $66,158$, $40,100$, and $50,363$, respectively.

B Training Details

Our models are trained using Fairseq.[9] As the data size for each language pair is relatively similar, oversampling is not implemented for MNMT. The dropout rate was set to 0.1, 0.4, and 0.3 for each dataset, and we use the Adam optimizer (Kingma and Ba, 2015) with a learning rate of 5e-4, 1e-3, and 5e-4, respectively, employing $4,000$ warm-up steps. The `Transformer-base` model was trained using four 32 GB V100 GPUs, and the `Transformer-big` model was trained using eight 32 GB V100 GPUs, with a batch size of $4,096$ tokens. To speed up training, mixed precision training (Micikevicius et al., 2018) is also employed. Each dataset is trained for 500, 200, and 500 epochs.

C Limitations

While this study proposed a novel method for improving neural interlingua representations for zero-shot translation, the following limitations should be addressed in future work:

- The inaccurate interlingua length predictor currently leads to inferior performance for translation from non-centric languages. Therefore, a better predictor should be explored to improve the performance.
- We used the length of centric language sentences as the interlingua length, which may limit the application for using parallel sentences not involving the centric language. Therefore, a better way to generate variable lengths for neural interlingua representations should be developed in future work.
- We have yet to test whether the neural interlingua representations obtained in this study can act as a semantic pivot among all the languages. Thus, it would be interesting to evaluate the effectiveness of our variable-length interlingua representations on cross-lingual language understanding tasks (Hu et al., 2020).

[7] `https://github.com/fxsjy/jieba`

[8] `https://github.com/moses-smt/mosesdecoder`

[9] `https://github.com/facebookresearch/fairseq`

Towards an Efficient Approach for Controllable Text Generation

Iván Martínez-Murillo, Paloma Moreda, Elena Lloret
Dept. of Software and Computing Systems
University of Alicante
Apdo. de Correos 99
E-03080, Alicante, Spain
{ivan.martinez, elena.lloret, moreda}@ua.es

Abstract

Since the emergence of Transformers architecture, the Natural Language Generation (NLG) field has advanced at breakneck speed. Large language models (LLMs) have achieved remarkable results in the field of generative artificial intelligence (AI). Nevertheless, they also present some problems worth analysing: not only are they computationally non-viable to academia, but they also have other issues, such us not generating text in a fully controllable way or the phenomenon known as hallucination. Because of this, the purpose of this paper is to outline and set the ideas for a new PhD thesis research. This PhD thesis will aim at advancing the state of the art by discovering new cost-effective, efficient and high-performing approaches to controlled text generation that could perform well in the different NLG tasks. Therefore, the main objective of this PhD thesis is to design a novel and efficient task-agnostic architecture that could obtain equivalent performance of LLMs, while generating text in a controllable way and including external commonsense knowledge.

1 Introduction

Natural language generation (NLG) field is the sub-field within natural language processing (NLP) area that generates natural language to meet a communicative goal (Reiter and Dale, 1997). Traditionally, there was a more classical and global vision about the NLG architecture that implied to divide generation in three stages: (1) macro-planning, (2) micro-planning and (3) surface realisation (Reiter and Dale, 1997). Later, neural networks caused a new trend in NLG, involving what we know nowadays as generative artificial intelligente (AI). Generative AI is a trend that encompasses systems that are constructed applying machine learning algorithms (Sun et al., 2022). Whitin this trend, Transformers (Vaswani et al., 2017) have revolutionised the NLG field owing to the concept of attention. Several proposals based on Transformers have been made, being Large Language Models (LLMs) the ones which better performance have achieved in tasks such as text summarisation or machine-translation, among others (Wolf et al., 2020). Despite this, these models present some issues worth commenting on. On the one hand, bests LLMs, such as GPT4 (estimated to have 1 trillion of parameters) (OpenAI, 2023) or LLaMa (65 billions of parameters) (Touvron et al., 2023) have a huge amount of parameters in their neural networks, which is only available to big companies, such as Google, due to the economic and temporary expense of training that models. On the other hand, these models do not generate text in a fully controlled way, leading to problems, such as hallucination or the lack of commonsense, among others. In fact, hallucination occurs even in the most superior LLMs such as GPT4 (Zhao et al., 2023). Figure 1 shows an example of hallucination in ChatGPT.

Because of this, the purpose of this paper is to set up the ideas for a new PhD thesis in which we will study and present a novel architecture that

[1]Tested in May, 2023

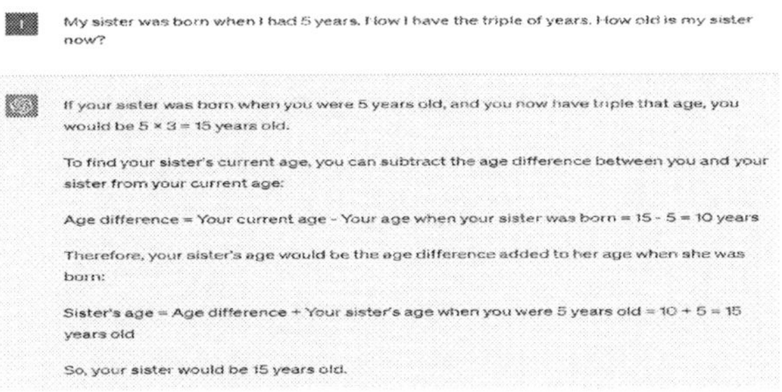

Figure 1: Hallucination example of ChatGPT [1]

could generate text in a more controlled manner, while being more efficient and less expensive. The proposed architecture will also include external commonsense knowledge with the aim of mitigating hallucination.

Therefore, the structure of this paper is organised in the following way: First of all, a commentary on the NLG background and the most common architectures are explained. Secondly, some research questions are introduced. Thirdly, the initial hypothesis about this PhD thesis and its corresponding objectives scheduled within a three years plan are set. Finally, a conclusion with the expected results of this thesis are presented.

2 Background

Research in NLG started by the end of 1970 (McDonald, 2010) and since then, it has advanced substantially. Depending on the type input, NLG can be traditionally classified into 2 main subgroups (Vicente et al., 2015): (1) text-to-text generation (T2T) and (2) data-to-text generation (D2T). Input data in D2T generation can adopt several types including images, voice, binary data, databases and knowledge. Recently, with the emergence of generative AI, the concept of (3) none-to-text is also introduced (Chandu and Black, 2020).

Other classifications are based on the task typology the generation system has been trained for. According to (Dong et al., 2022), NLG tasks are divided into three classes:

1. Text abbreviation: These tasks are devoted to detect the most relevant information in a text and condense that information into a short text, such as text summarization or question generation.

2. Text expansion: These tasks aim at generate completing sentences or texts from some meaningful words. Short text expansion and topic-to-essay generation are examples of this type of task.

3. Text rewriting and reasoning: These task work towards rewriting text into another style or applying reasoning methods, e.g. text style transfer and dialogue generation.

To achieve the communicative goal of the aforementioned tasks, several types of architectures have been proposed along this time. Based on the existing literature concerning NLG, some key papers proposing these architectures have been selected and have been represented in a temporal timeline. Figure 3 shows the evolution of architecture trends in NLG. These architectures can be grouped into three main categories (Gatt and Krahmer, 2018):

1. Modular architectures: This type of architectures follow a sequential scheme, which makes a clear distinction between distinct sub-tasks. The most popular modular architecture was proposed by Reiter (1994), which consists in a pipeline of three phases plus one optional phase, where the input into a sub-task is the output of the preceding sub-task. Figure 2 shows the different sub-tasks in the classical modular architecture.

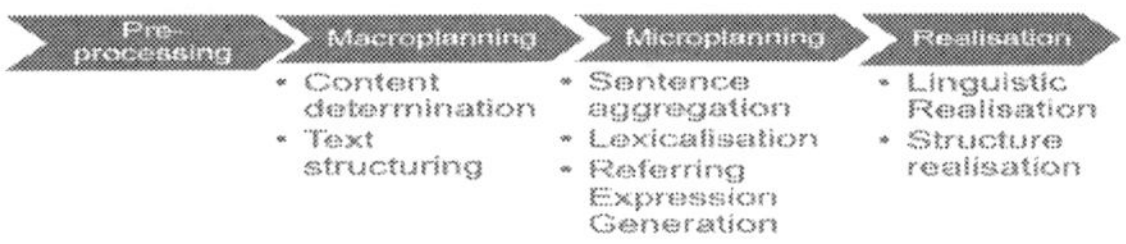

Figure 2: Sub-task division in the modular architecture for the stages proposed by (Reiter and Dale, 1997)

Some examples of this type of architectures can be found in (Mann and Moore, 1981), (Hovy, 1987), (Levelt, 1989), (Nirenburg et al., 1989) and (Reiter, 1994).

2. Planning perspectives: This type of architectures have a similar sub-task division similar to modular architectures, but they are more flexible owing to they allow to combine two or more consecutive sub-tasks into the same task. An example of this combination is to perform text structuring and sentence aggregation sub-tasks in the same tasks. Within this group, some examples of approaches that could be highlighted can be found in (Fikes and Nilsson, 1971), (Appelt, 1985), (Hovy, 1991), (Bateman, 1997),(Koller and Stone, 2007), (Rieser and Lemon, 2009), (Nakatsu and White, 2010) and (Lemon, 2011).

3. Global approaches: This type of architectures do not distinguish between sub-tasks, performing the entire generation process in a single task, having a strong reliance on statistical learn-

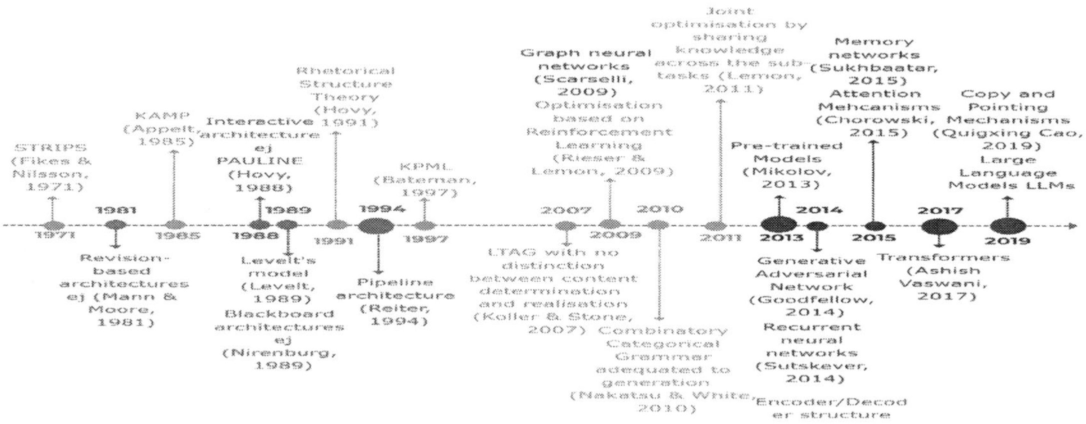

Figure 3: Timeline of NLG architectures (modular architectures in blue, planning perspectives in light blue, and global approaches in dark blue).

ing. Transformers (Vaswani et al., 2017) are an example of architecture within this category. With an encoder/decoder structure and an attention mechanism (Chorowski et al., 2015), Transformers and LLMs have revolutionised the NLG field. Research works that fall under this group are: Graph Neural Networks (Scarselli et al., 2008), Generative Adversarial Nets (Mirza et al., 2014), Recurrent Neural Networks (Sutskever et al., 2014), Pre-trained Models (Mikolov et al., 2013), Memory Networks (Sukhbaatar et al., 2015) and Copy and Pointing Mechanism (See et al., 2017). However, they also present some problems, as mentioned in Section 1.

Considering these problems, there is still some promising future directions to enhance text generation models. Some of the future directions in which this PhD thesis will focus are suggested in the following section.

3 Open Research Questions

In order to advance towards an efficient approach for controllable text generation that can overcome the drawbacks state-of-the-art architectures have, several research questions are suggested and discussed.

What is controllable text generation, and what are the most common techniques to address it? Controllable text generation is the task of generating natural language whose attributes can be controlled (Prabhumoye et al., 2020). These attributes can be stylistics (politeness, sentiment, etc), based on the demographic attributes of the interlocutor (age, gender, etc), or based on the content (including some keywords, entities, order of information, etc).

In order to control text generation, there are three main strategies (Erdem et al., 2022):

1. Via hyperparameters: Language models are trained with huge amounts of texts, which maybe cause that training data is unbalanced. Controlling the generation by hyperparameters could help the model to do a better generalisation of knowledge.

2. Via additional input: This group of methods consist on fine-tuning pre-trained models with additional input in order to adapt a pre-trained model to have a good performance in a more specific.

3. Via conditional training: This term refers to the group of training methods that utilise internal control variables that enrich the generation with specific capabilities.

During development of this PhD thesis, I will study and combine all three groups of approaches to propose a model that could produce text in a controllable way.

What is hallucination, what causes hallucination and which are the best ways to mitigate it? Hallucination in NLG refers to a text generated by a NLG model that is nonsensical or unfaithful to the provided source input (Ji et al., 2023). There are two categories of hallucinations: *intrinsic hallucinations* when the generated text refutes the input text, and *extrinsic hallucinations* when the generated text cannot be proved by the input.

Hallucination can be caused at two stages of the generation: both during the construction of datasets which may contain source-reference divergences, and during the training and inference step caused by the incomprehension to represent information in the encoder and decoder.

To solve this, there are some ways to keep hallucination at a low level. First of all, creating a faithful dataset, or automatically cleaning data from existing datasets. Secondly, by altering the structure of encoders and decoders to make them interpret semantics of the input in a better way. Thirdly, by proposing an optimal training strategy such as reinforcement learning or controllable generation. Finally, including external commonsense knowledge could help the model to mitigate hallucination. This PhD thesis will focus on the analysis of controllable generation techniques to reduce hallucination along with inclusion of external commonsense knowledge.

Is is possible to obtain an architecture that performs equally to LLMs without being as computationally demanding as them? Recently, LLMs have been the most hot topic in the NLG area, achieving a high performance in most of the latest models such as GPT4 (OpenAI, 2023), LLaMa (Touvron et al., 2023) and BLOOM (Scao et al., 2022), among others. Nevertheless, they have one major inconvenient. The time and computational expense needed to train these models are inaccessible to academia, as mentioned in Section 1. Thus, this PhD thesis will analyse and propose cost-effective architectures that could approximate LLMs performance and also solving some issues these models have.

Is there a task-agnostic architecture able to perform well for different tasks? Most of researches in the NLG area are focused on a specific task that while they perform correctly in one task, they underperform in others. Thus, this study will analyse most common task-agnostic techniques in order to propose a model that could achieve a high performance at every task.

4 Objectives

Given the research questions defined in Section 3 that we aim to cover in this thesis, our initial objective is that a cost-effective and efficient NLG approach that implements controllable text generation techniques along with external commonsense knowledge will help to mitigate the problem of hallucination, without worsening the results compared to the best-performing state-of-the-art models and will be able to perform well in different generation tasks.

To complete this objective, the following tasks with its corresponding schedule along three years have been proposed, as it can be seen in Figure 4. The schedule is divided in three sub-groups. In *Group A* the state-of-the-art will be studied. In *group B* an architecture will be proposed and tested. Finally, in *group C* the proposed architecture will be adapted to different NLG tasks.

A1. To analyse the state-of-the-art focused on controllable text generation techniques.

A2. To analyse the state-of-the-art focused on hallucination mitigation techniques.

A3. To analyse the state-of–the-art focused on task-agnostic architectures.

B1. To compare the performance of open-source state-of-the-art architectures using a common benchmark.

B2. To propose a cost-effective architecture that can generate text in a controllable way.

B3. To evaluate the performance of the proposed architecture against state-of-the-art architectures.

C1. To adapt the architecture to some of NLG tasks, e.g., summarisation or text simplification.

C2. To compare results with some architectures oriented to a specific task.

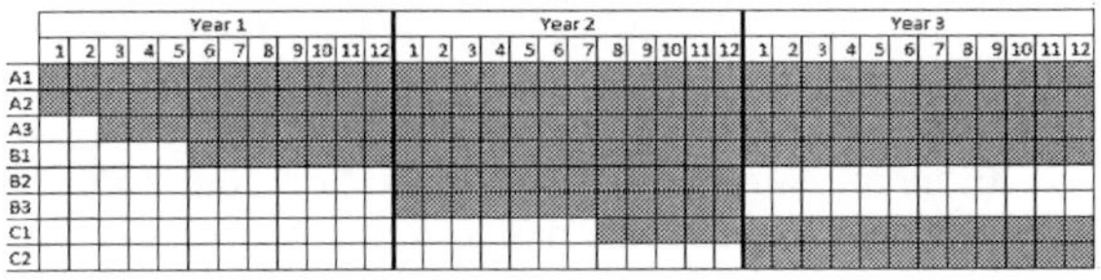

Figure 4: PhD thesis schedule

5 Conclusion

In spite of the great performance LLMs have for NLG, they also present some drawbacks. Thus, there is some room for improvement to advance scientific knowledge in NLG. In light of this, the objective of this PhD thesis is to find a more efficient architecture that could produce text in a controllable way and mitigate as much as possible the phenomena known as hallucination as much as possible by exploiting the use of external commonsense knowledge. Once an architecture is defined, this line of work will focus on adapting that architecture to achieve a cost-effective performance in some NLG tasks, and measuring that performance. We expect to obtain similar and comparable results to state-of-the-art models, but solving the issue of hallucination while using an efficient model that will help to reduce the carbon footprint.

Acknowledgements

This work has been funded by the European Commission ICT COST Action "Multi-task, Multilingual, Multi-modal Language Generation" (CA18231). In addition, the research work conducted is part of the R&D projects "CORTEX: Conscious Text Generation" (PID2021-123956OB-I00), funded by MCIN/ AEI/10.13039/501100011033/ and by "ERDF A way of making Europe"; "CLEAR.TEXT:Enhancing the modernization public sector organizations by deploying Natural Language Processing to make their digital content CLEARER to those with cognitive disabilities" (TED2021-130707B-I00), funded by MCIN/AEI/10.13039/501100011033 and "European Union NextGenerationEU/PRTR"; and the project "NL4DISMIS: Natural Language Technologies for dealing with dis- and misinformation with grant reference (CIPROM/2021/21)" funded by the Generalitat Valenciana.

References

Appelt, DE. 1985. Planning english sentences. cambridge university press.

Bateman, John A. 1997. Enabling technology for multilingual natural language generation: the kpml development environment. *Natural Language Engineering*, 3(1):15–55.

Chandu, Khyathi Raghavi and Alan W Black. 2020. Positioning yourself in the maze of neural text generation: A task-agnostic survey.

Chorowski, Jan K, Dzmitry Bahdanau, Dmitriy Serdyuk, Kyunghyun Cho, and Yoshua Bengio. 2015. Attention-based models for speech recognition. *Advances in neural information processing systems*, 28.

Dong, Chenhe, Yinghui Li, Haifan Gong, Miaoxin Chen, Junxin Li, Ying Shen, and Min Yang. 2022. A survey of natural language generation. *ACM Comput. Surv.*, 55(8), dec.

Erdem, Erkut, Menekse Kuyu, Semih Yagcioglu, Anette Frank, Letitia Parcalabescu, Barbara Plank, Andrii Babii, Oleksii Turuta, Aykut Erdem, Iacer Calixto, et al. 2022. Neural natural language generation: A survey on multilinguality, multimodality, controllability and learning. *Journal of Artificial Intelligence Research*, 73:1131–1207.

Fikes, Richard E and Nils J Nilsson. 1971. Strips: A new approach to the application of theorem proving to problem solving. *Artificial intelligence*, 2(3-4):189–208.

Gatt, Albert and Emiel Krahmer. 2018. Survey of the state of the art in natural language generation: Core tasks, applications and evaluation.

Hovy, Eduard. 1987. Generating natural language under pragmatic constraints. *Journal of Pragmatics*, 11(6):689–719.

Hovy, Eduard H. 1991. *Approaches to the planning of coherent text*. Springer.

Ji, Ziwei, Nayeon Lee, Rita Frieske, Tiezheng Yu, Dan Su, Yan Xu, Etsuko Ishii, Ye Jin Bang, Andrea Madotto, and Pascale Fung. 2023. Survey of hallucination in natural language generation. *ACM Comput. Surv.*, 55(12), mar.

Koller, Alexander and Matthew Stone. 2007. Sentence generation as a planning problem. In *Proceedings of the 45th Annual Meeting of the Association of Computational Linguistics*, pages 336–343, Prague, Czech Republic, June. Association for Computational Linguistics.

Lemon, Oliver. 2011. Learning what to say and how to say it: Joint optimisation of spoken dialogue management and natural language generation. *Computer Speech & Language*, 25(2):210–221.

Levelt, W. 1989. Speaking: From intention to articulation mit press. *Cambridge, MA*.

Mann, William C and James A Moore. 1981. Computer generation of multiparagraph english text. *American Journal of Computational Linguistics*, 7(1):17–29.

McDonald, David D. 2010. Natural language generation. *Handbook of natural language processing*, 2:121–144.

Mikolov, Tomas, Ilya Sutskever, Kai Chen, Greg S Corrado, and Jeff Dean. 2013. Distributed representations of words and phrases and their compositionality. *Advances in neural information processing systems*, 26.

Mirza, Mehdi, Bing Xu, David Warde-Farley, Sherjil Ozair, Aaron Courville, Yoshua Bengio, Ian J Goodfellow, and Jean Pouget-Abadie. 2014. Generative adversarial nets. *Advances in neural information processing systems*, 27:2672–2680.

Nakatsu, Crystal and Michael White. 2010. Generating with discourse combinatory categorial grammar. *Linguistic Issues in Language Technology*, 4.

Nirenburg, Sergei, Victor R Lesser, and Eric Nyberg. 1989. Controlling a language generation planner. In *IJCAI*, pages 1524–1530.

OpenAI. 2023. Gpt-4 technical report.

Prabhumoye, Shrimai, Alan W Black, and Ruslan Salakhutdinov. 2020. Exploring controllable text generation techniques. In *Proceedings of the 28th*

International Conference on Computational Linguistics, pages 1–14, Barcelona, Spain (Online), December. International Committee on Computational Linguistics.

Reiter, Ehud and Robert Dale. 1997. Building applied natural language generation systems. *Natural Language Engineering*, 3(1):57–87.

Reiter, Ehud. 1994. Has a consensus nl generation architecture appeared, and is it psycholinguistically plausible?

Rieser, Verena and Oliver Lemon. 2009. Natural language generation as planning under uncertainty for spoken dialogue systems. *Empirical Methods in Natural Language Generation: Data-oriented Methods and Empirical Evaluation*, pages 105–120.

Scao, Teven Le, Angela Fan, Christopher Akiki, Ellie Pavlick, Suzana Ilić, Daniel Hesslow, Roman Castagné, Alexandra Sasha Luccioni, François Yvon, Matthias Gallé, et al. 2022. Bloom: A 176b-parameter open-access multilingual language model. *arXiv preprint arXiv:2211.05100.*

Scarselli, Franco, Marco Gori, Ah Chung Tsoi, Markus Hagenbuchner, and Gabriele Monfardini. 2008. The graph neural network model. *IEEE transactions on neural networks*, 20(1):61–80.

See, Abigail, Peter J Liu, and Christopher D Manning. 2017. Get to the point: Summarization with pointer-generator networks. *arXiv preprint arXiv:1704.04368.*

Sukhbaatar, Sainbayar, Jason Weston, Rob Fergus, et al. 2015. End-to-end memory networks. *Advances in neural information processing systems*, 28.

Sun, Jiao, Q Vera Liao, Michael Muller, Mayank Agarwal, Stephanie Houde, Kartik Talamadupula, and Justin D Weisz. 2022. Investigating explainability of generative ai for code through scenario-based design. In *27th International Conference on Intelligent User Interfaces*, pages 212–228.

Sutskever, Ilya, Oriol Vinyals, and Quoc V Le. 2014. Sequence to sequence learning with neural networks. *Advances in neural information processing systems*, 27.

Touvron, Hugo, Thibaut Lavril, Gautier Izacard, Xavier Martinet, Marie-Anne Lachaux, Timothée Lacroix, Baptiste Rozière, Naman Goyal, Eric Hambro, Faisal Azhar, Aurelien Rodriguez, Armand Joulin, Edouard Grave, and Guillaume Lample. 2023. Llama: Open and efficient foundation language models.

Vaswani, Ashish, Noam Shazeer, Niki Parmar, Jakob Uszkoreit, Llion Jones, Aidan N. Gomez, Lukasz Kaiser, and Illia Polosukhin. 2017. Attention is all you need.

Vicente, Marta, Cristina Barros, Fernando S Peregrino, Francisco Agulló, and Elena Lloret. 2015. La generación de lenguaje natural: análisis del estado actual. *Computación y Sistemas*, 19(4):721–756.

Wolf, Thomas, Lysandre Debut, Victor Sanh, Julien Chaumond, Clement Delangue, Anthony Moi, Pierric Cistac, Tim Rault, Rémi Louf, Morgan Funtowicz, Joe Davison, Sam Shleifer, Patrick von Platen, Clara Ma, Yacine Jernite, Julien Plu, Canwen Xu, Teven Le Scao, Sylvain Gugger, Mariama Drame, Quentin Lhoest, and Alexander M. Rush. 2020. Transformers: State-of-the-art natural language processing. In *Proceedings of the 2020 Conference on Empirical Methods in Natural Language Processing: System Demonstrations*, pages 38–45, Online, October. Association for Computational Linguistics.

Zhao, Wayne Xin, Kun Zhou, Junyi Li, Tianyi Tang, Xiaolei Wang, Yupeng Hou, Yingqian Min, Beichen Zhang, Junjie Zhang, Zican Dong, et al. 2023. A survey of large language models. *arXiv preprint arXiv:2303.18223.*

Natural Language Generation in the Logos Model

Sara Amato
Independent Scholar, Italy
saraamato11@gmail.com

Kutz Arrieta
Independent Scholar, USA
kutzaki@gmail.com

Abstract

In this paper, we focus on the generation module in the Logos Model and, more generally, target modules via generation-specific linguistic challenges, illustrating them with examples taken from Italian and Spanish as target languages. We briefly explore the different models and applications in existence for Natural Language Generation as context for the description of the Logos Machine Translation Model.

1 Introduction

Natural Language Generation has a long tradition in the field of Computational Linguistics. It can be defined as the means and methods to produce human language, be it from another language, from coded instructions, from graphical representations or from datasets. The modules to be included in a generation component will vary greatly depending on the methods used to produce natural language.

Much has changed in the field since the Logos Model was active as a commercial system. It is beyond the scope of this paper to provide a review of those changes. The release of Large Language Models (LLMs) to the public in the last few months is shifting the research and development paradigm for Natural Language Processing and Generation. There is much to say about LLMs. Here we just want to bring the reader's attention to the term "Generative AI". In its most basic sense, Generative AI (Artificial Intelligence) is a type of artificial intelligence technology that can produce various types of content including text, imagery and audio. It produces synthetic data (computer-generated content). This is exactly what Natural Language Generation does. What differs is the methodology. In this paper we focus on a methodology that has nothing to do with Generative AI in its current meaning.

There are products, applications and research prototypes that deal with the task of generating human language from data. Some of these have as their final product biographies or résumés; others produce reports of different types. One aspect that is shared by these different Natural Language Generation (NLG) applications is that some type of parsing (natural language processing) is involved. One doesn't go from data "straight" to generation. Instead, data needs to be analyzed for relevance and classified, and then facts and factoids (in Natural Language Processing (NLP) factoids are small information units about the world) need to be extracted. In this view, the data needs to be understood before any kind of language generation can occur.

Other initiatives have tried to convert schemata or different types of graphic representations into human language. In this case also, the schema needs to be understood first, to be "parsed," before generation occurs. Between the steps of parsing and generation, several other modules might be present, such as sentence planners or tag classifiers. These modules are usually preceded by information planning modules.

Here, we are focusing on language generation in the context of Machine Translation, more specifically, in the Logos Model. The Logos Model is mostly based on linguistic knowledge, both syntax and semantics, supported by semantic and world knowledge encoded in a knowledge graph and a relational database.

2 Types of Generation

As mentioned in Section 1, generation is realized in different ways depending on the restrictions or potential of the system at hand, and on the application for which it is intended. In the remainder of Section 2 we mention some of these applications.

Sections 3 and 4 describe generation in the Logos Model through examples. We conclude in section 5.

2.1 Applications

Generation is used to build well-formed sentences from basic meaning components. From something like *someone has children*, the user chooses from options such as sentence focus, gender of the speaker, etc. This is the case of Phrasomatic, for example.

Generation may be used to create language models that are easily understood by humans not requiring them to have specific knowledge of a certain domain. Håkan Burden and Rogardt Heldal, in the context of Model-Driven Engineering, have experimented with the use of Natural Language Generation to go from a Platform-Independent Model (PIM) to a Computational Independent Model (CIM) using Grammatical Framework. The result is a description of the original software model as well as the underlying motivations for design decisions, in the form of natural language texts.

Generation may be used to generate reports from data sets, such as in the proposal from Arria. The idea is to save time for users who need to analyze large amounts of data, such as finance portfolios.

Generation may be used to produce both questions and explanations from Natural Language understanding and reasoning systems. This is the case of products such as KnowMatters or IBM Watson.

For all the cases aforementioned, different approaches to natural language are used. Some are unification-based solutions, such as Tree-Adjoining Grammars (TAGs), etc., but we will not go into detailed descriptions of these systems, since our goal here is to describe the Logos approach to generation.

2.2 Models

In Machine Translation (MT) systems based solely on statistical or neural models, there is no, or very limited, semantic generation. Statistical MT systems match patterns in aligned bilingual texts to build a statistical model of translation. This has nothing to do with the tasks of parsing and generation in systems based on linguistic knowledge.

Dependency Grammars have been and are being used in several models. In these models, sentence generation is viewed as a sequence of transductions (surface representations), produced by different grammars.

The Universal Networking Language (UNL) has also been used as a tool in generation systems. Logos uses its own semantico-syntactic abstraction language (SAL) throughout its modules.

In some systems, generation starts with some type of logical representation by projecting a "general" syntactic structure. After this, generation rules apply and produce the desired output in the target language.

We should mention here some methods and projects which are, akin to the Logos Model, knowledge- and rule- based such as the Wikimedia Abstract Language Project. In this project LLMs are not being adopted because the main goal is to make it possible for less-resourced languages to generate content and the assumption is that those languages do not have enough digital content for the models to be trained on. Worth mentioning here also is the work from Maria Keet and her team in University of Cape Town on isiZulu languages.

3 Natural Language Generation in Logos

The Logos model is described in detail elsewhere (Scott 2003 et al.). We will not repeat such detailed descriptions here, but we include just enough of how the Logos model works to better understand where and when generation happens.

We should mention, though, that most of what has been written about the Logos model deals with source analysis. Very little has been written about its Generation module, often referred to as Target Generation.

There seems to be some kind of "exhaustion effect" when it comes to generation: tokenization, resolution, lexical matches, relation to source syntactic and semantic parsing, etc. Several extremely important things need to happen before going into Generation. But the application has to decide clause boundaries and dependencies, resolve ambiguities, group phrases, understand phrase dependencies, etc., in order to provide the Generation module with the most precise information possible.

Everyone in MT is aware of the importance of generation. After all, it is what the user first sees: how "good" the system is at producing a language that mimics native speaker abilities. But the next and more important factor for the user is how close the target is to the source, how faithfully it reflects the information provided in the source language. In addition, there is a good variety of editing tools, and thus, it makes sense to put most of your energy in source analysis and provide the Generation module with just what it needs to produce an acceptable output that can easily be edited. So, Logos adopted the correct strategy in regards to the distribution of resources in the model.

Nevertheless, greater independence between source and target modules was being planned to make it perfect in every possible aspect and to increase its modularity.

3.1 Description

The Generation or target module is described in Scott 2003, but let's list here its main features.

The TRAN label refers to phases in the syntactic and semantic parsing and generation pipeline. Generation does not start in TRAN4, even though it is considered the most "generation-like" TRAN. TRAN4 is the final stage in the generation pipeline. In TRAN1 we already have rewrite rules (rules that transform source language structures into target language structures). Some of the behaviors of generation rules are directly controlled by source analysis rules. Source analysis triggers generation rules. While rewrite rules occur early in the translation process, they are not considered "pure" generation. "Authentic" generation rules occur in TRAN4. These rules are quite complex (often more so than source rules). TRAN4 builds well-formed sentences in the target language. TRAN4 and, therefore, the generation module, is supposed to be multi-source, and should not depend on the particular source analysis of one specific language or another. It is based on an abstract representation or interlingua.

The semantico-syntactic (SAL) representation that Logos uses to encode languages and rules is an important asset for Generation. In the end, the Logos model has proved very successful in understanding that a higher level of abstraction is required when coding and classifying parts of speech, which goes beyond the usual part of speech classifications (nouns, adjectives, etc.). The Logos classification, based on this higher level of abstraction, reflects something that we could call the deep semantic functionality of each part of speech, whereby different members of a word class belong to a similar semantic category provided that they trigger similar syntactic behavior: *send* and *give* have identical chains of semantico-syntactic codes (manually assigned in the knowledge graph) because a) their deep semantics calls for a second indirect object and b) the indirect object can be introduced by the preposition *to* when following the direct object (*he gave a camera to his wife*) or by no preposition at all by inverting the order of the two objects (*he gave his wife a camera*). The verb *communicate*, instead, shares only part of its semantico-syntactic chain with *send* and *give*, because its syntactic environment only shares with them a) but not b). When looking at Logos SAL coding we see a representation that mimics what happens in our brains when processing natural languages.

Target rules are part of the generation module. Target is produced incrementally. Morphological and semantic information in the lexicon often encodes features needed in target generation. We would like to highlight here that the morphological modules in the Logos model, even though seldom described, are a great feature of the model. In some sense, the morphological modules in Logos are also "mixed" in the sense of parsing and generation. These modules need to encode all the information necessary to function for both a source and a target language. In parsing systems the morphological modules only need to take into account analysis cases; they don't need to restrict "overgeneration," as it is assumed that spurious tokens should not occur in the input. When a morphology module is to be used for both parsing and generation, the rules need to be much more precise to avoid spurious tokens in both directions. When building a morphology module for a parsing-only system, rules can generalize surface token to lemma rules, assuming the spurious surface form will not appear in text, and if it did, it would not morph to any valid lemmas.

The challenges when building morphological components for parsing or for generation are quite different. The fact that the design of the model allows for the morphological components to be used in both directions leaves very little room for "free rides", i.e. situations where possible counter-cases do not arise, such as morphology parsing, where spurious forms would not be part of the data to be parsed.

For example, in a morphology for analysis one could write a rule for any clitic and any number of clitics to be attached to a Spanish verb in the gerund or infinitive form, assuming a text written in Spanish will not have combinations not allowed. This is to say that in the process of parsing one can assume that no spurious combinations will be present. While, if the morphology is to be capable of generating forms in Spanish, more complex rules must be written to allow only grammatical combinations of clitics and verbs and prevent over-generation.

In the transfer phase, parse and generation, the source tree is built and rebuilt through its source analysis while accommodating the needs of the target language. The Logos Model uses TRAN rules. These are syntactic rules rooted in the semantics of the components or entities. TRAN rules are target or group-specific, and they call target-specific tables

(30-tables, 40-tables and 50-tables). These tables accomplish different tasks, getting more and more specific to a given target as the pipeline progresses. After this, the generation phase takes place, where constituent movement, lexical selection and final formatting take place.

3.2 Evolution of the Model

The Logos model has been evolving since its conception. As mentioned before, the last phase of this evolution was aiming at a greater separation of source and target modules.

It has not been easy to classify Logos among the MT systems because of the partial separation of parse and generation, the transfer modules, the shared semantic rules and the use of an abstract representation (SAL). For its design to move toward a full interlingua model, source and target language need to be more independent of each other while maintaining the complex lexicon structure and SAL language, which allows for a semantico-syntactic representation of knowledge through Natural Language representation. This change in design is motivated by the need for modularity in order to improve results and to accelerate the addition of new language pairs. This change was started but has not been completed. In this new design all source operations are completed independently of the target language, and target languages need only to concentrate on generation from a SAL parse tree, without any concern of impact on the source language parse or on other target languages.

4 Linguistic Challenges in Generation

In this section we discuss some of the challenges Generation modules face. These are challenges that any system needs to address and solve in order to produce the correct results.

4.1 Verb Phrases and Verb Compounds

Generation of verb compounds and phrases is addressed in SemTab rules that are specific to a language pair. SemTab is explained elsewhere (e.g. Scott 2018); here we see some examples where SemTab rules handle "verb + particle" structures.

1. LOOK (VI) OUT (PART) = TENER CUIDADO
2. LET (VT) OFF (PART) = DESPEDIR

After the RES (resolution) module has resolved that an element is a particle and not a preposition or an adverb, for example, the combination of the "verb + particle" strings in a rule represents a different verb, with a different semantico-syntactic code from the one assigned to the original main verb, and a different transfer in the target language.

4.2 Semantic Context

In the case of the "verb + noun rule" exemplified here, we are taking a set of nouns that belong to a certain semantic category and handling the combination of the copulative verb and any of these nouns, under any form or any modification context, as an idiom. Therefore, the translation should be tailored to the target language.

3. BE (VI) (UNITS OF LINEAR MSR-PREC BY ARITHMATE) = MEDIR N

In German source, separable verb prefixes and particles must be reassigned to the verb so that they can be handled as a single string. In a sequence like: *Wir drehen weiter* each word enters the translation module separately. Therefore *drehen* and *weiter* would, by default, be handled separately. Once RES confirms that *weiter* should be treated as a separable particle there will be a match on rules like:

4. DREHEN WEITER = CONTINUARE A GIRARE

This rule re-codes the verb *drehen* as the verb *weiterdrehen* to allow a match on another very generic SemTab rule coded for *weiterdrehen*, which will generate the appropriate translation in Italian.

5. WEITERDREHEN N = CONTINUARE A GIRARE N

This module, even though not a part of Generation per se, is a very elegant way to handle these types of transformations.

4.3 Adverb Generation: Form and Position

Adverbs play an important role and are often difficult to generate correctly. They have syntactic scope, therefore, their position in the target sentence is syntactically relevant and they take different shapes.

6. EN - errantly

   ES - de manera errante

   IT - a casaccio

In the case of the adverb in example 6, we do not want to generate the default *errantemente* through the lexicon and/or the morphology in every case. *-ly* adverbs in English cannot be treated equally, depending on their semantics and their position in the sentence, the Generation module needs to treat them differently. Adverbs such as *roughly, generally* and *slowly* do not belong to the same semantic category. *Slowly* is the default case as *-ly* (or *-mente*) derivationally creates adverbs of manner from adjectives, while *roughly* is more a modifier than an adverb of manner.

4.4 Quantifiers

Parsing quantifiers presents serious challenges. Generating the appropriate quantifiers in the target language is not trivial. Quantifiers are another example of several semantic and syntactic complex issues in which the design of the parse has to either be "complete" or take into account the needs of the target languages.

7. EN - *any two books*

   ES - *dos libros cualesquiera*

The default transfer for this phrase would have been **cualquier dos libros*, but a TRAN rule, dealing with the source noun phrase analysis and sending a signal to the transfer module causes the Generation module to effect the correct output. Therefore, in these cases, as in many, source analysis and target generation are intertwined.

4.5 Clitics

Pronominal clitics in Romance languages are extremely difficult to handle in an NLP application. By comparison with other systems, Logos performs very well, as all the information needed to choose between **le** and **con él**, etc. in different contexts is provided in the source analysis.

8. EN - *You may contact him*

   ES - *puede contactarle*

The Logos Model produces: ES**:** *se puede poner en comunicación con él*

As we see in the example both outputs are correct, as *puede contactar con él* would have been, but it is a challenge to decide which should be the default strategy: attached clitic or preposition + pronoun?

In this specific example, a SemTab rule is making the decision:

9. CONTACT (VT-ACTIVE) N (NOM-HUMAN) N = N PONERSE(REFL) EN COMUNICACIÓN CON N

We should note here that Logos in its design allows for very creative and productive strategies. The "black hole" strategy, initially conceived for dealing with clitics in Spanish, is a good example of this. For example, a verb in English might be translated by a verb phrase in Spanish. For example, *to stock → almacenar en el sótano*. If you decide in Generation to attach your clitic at the end of the verb phrase, you would get ungrammatical outputs such as **quiero almacenar en el sótanolo* because the system sees the string *almacenar en el sótano* as the verb transfer in Spanish and attaches the clitic at the end.

There were several ways this could be handled in-house, but, since Logos allowed its users to have proprietary dictionaries, the question of how to solve this in a systematic and predictable way arose. Every verb phrase of more than one word in Italian or Spanish may have a black hole, and the Generation rules ask the verb: "Do you have a black hole?" If true, the clitic goes into the black hole (located just after the head of the verb phrase). If false, it attaches at the end of the verb. This results in huge improvements for Generation. These black holes can also be used in noun phrases, adjectival phrases, etc.

Let us consider the English verb *ask,* which is translated in Italian by the verb *chiedere.* You may decide to attach the clitic at the end of the verb like in *ask him → chiedetegli* or to place the pronoun before the verb at the beginning of the clause like in *you may ask him → gli potete chiedere.* When the clitic is loaded at the end of the verb phrase, and the verb phrase is complex, the exact same behavior described in Spanish occurs in Italian: *you can always give it to your teacher → lo potete sempre dare al vostro insegnante.*

4.6 –ed in English

Another big group of Generation challenges are the *-ed* verb forms in English and their translation in Spanish and Italian.

10. EN - *The file is displayed by John*

    ES - *John visualiza el fichero*

    IT - *John visualizza il file*

11. EN - *The file is displayed by clicking the mouse*

    ES - *Se visualiza el fichero chasqueando el ratón*

    IT - *Si visualizza il file cliccando sul mouse*

12. EN - *English is spoken here*

    ES - *Aquí se habla inglés*

    IT - *Qui si parla inglese*

English makes a very different usage of resultatives and passives as compared with Romance languages. The Generation module has to decide if the appropriate outcome is to transform the sentence into its active counterpart, maintain a passive or generate an impersonal sentence, among others. If the source parsing doesn't carry enough information (information that may not be needed for parsing per se), the Generation module cannot make the correct decision. The Logos Model handled these challenges well.

TRAN4 through its rules and tables determines if the noun phrase that follows *by* is really an agent and sends a signal. If it is an agent, the outcome in Spanish will be an active sentence (*John visualiza el fichero*). If it is not, it will be rendered as an instrumental in the target (**Se visualiza el fichero chasqueando al ratón*). Note the incorrect *al* in this sentence, probably due to a rule too powerful dealing with accusative animate complements in Spanish.

In other cases, and again through signals, in this case adapted to the needs of the target, the system will output an impersonal sentence (*Aquí se habla inglés*).

Italian exhibits similar behavior:

13. EN - *The file is displayed by John*

    IT - *John visualizza il file*

14. EN - *The file is displayed by clicking the mouse*

    IT - *Si visualizza il file cliccando sul mouse*

15. EN - *English is spoken here*

    IT - *Qui si parla inglese*

4.7 ser and estar / essere and stare

Spanish and Italian have two verbs to be, *ser* and *estar*, *essere* and *stare*. Deciding which one to use presents a great challenge for human learners of the language. To encode this distinction in a Generation system is as much of a challenge. For this, Logos implements a strategy that makes use of almost every module in the system. This is another one of those cases where the distinction between source analysis and target generation is really blurry. The Generation module needs great amounts of information from the source to make the decision. This information is not actually needed for the parse and it might not be needed for other target languages. Therefore, this need is encumbering the source analysis modules with a considerable amount of additional work.

We are ignoring here the idiomatic cases where the English verb is to be is translated by a completely different verb in Spanish (*be five meters long* → *medir cinco metros*).

16. EN - *I am dead*

    ES - *estoy muerto*

Choosing the verb *estar* in Spanish occurs in SemTab, before TRAN4. *ser* and *estar* rules in TRAN4 will check if there has been a match in SemTab and the issue has been solved. In that case, TRAN4 will not do anything.

17. BE (VI) ADJ (DEAD) = ESTAR ADJ (MUERTO)

    EN - *I am a dead horse*

    ES - *soy un caballo inactivo*

Source analysis knows that *dead* is modifying *horse* and not referring to the subject and, therefore the SemTab rule won't apply. TRAN4 runs all the necessary checks to make sure *ser* is the correct choice.

18. EN - *I am yellow*

    ES - *soy amarillo*

In TRAN4 the conditions for *estar* are not met, it is a basic predicative adjective, therefore, we chose the default case: *ser*. But, as we know, both are possible, but have different meanings (*soy amarillo* and *estoy amarillo*), but without any further modification in the sentence (*estoy amarillo de rabia*) or contextual information, the correct call is to use *ser*.

19. EN - *I am tired*

    ES - **se me cansa*

The correct output would be *estoy cansado*. Note that *tired* is a verbal adjective. Yet another example of the dependency between source and target. This small sentence is not analyzed correctly in the source and it is nearly impossible for the Generation module to recuperate from this. It should be noted that most of these nearly idiomatic cases are easily handled nowadays in other models such as statistical machine translation.

4.8 Existentials

Existentials, such as *there is* or *there are* in English are well known MT challenges.

20. EN - *There are toys here*

    ES - *Hay juguetes aquí*

21. EN - *There are broken toys here*

    ES - **está roto los juguetes aquí allí*

    ES - *Hay juguetes rotos aquí*

The system tries to match in SemTab rules such as:

22. BE ADV (HERE) = ESTAR ADV

But TRAN4 signals the system that we are dealing with an existential and therefore, *hay* must be produced. In the second case, this interaction fails and the system already in TRAN3 has misidentified the *–ed* (*broken*) as a resultative and *there* as a spatial adverb. Even though the model exhibits a great deal of flexibility by which one can recuperate from incorrect parses, it is not always done.

Not all shortcomings in the Logos Model should be understood as limitations of the design or the technology. If it had been an academic system maybe we would expect it to accommodate academic quality measure requirements, but it was a commercial system and, therefore, the measures of goodness are different. A commercial system is concerned with efficiency, cost, time to market, etc., while an academic system is not.

4.9 Ellipsis and other Special Cases

Sometimes the source languages allow certain ellipses that the target might not. The missing components have to be retrieved. These issues can be easily fixed in Logos.

23. EN - *If necessary*

    ES - *si fuera necesario*

Apparently harmless lexical entries such as *just* can stir a great amount of trouble. In some cases it is just an adverb, in others it is part of a verbal structure that needs to be rendered as such in the target. In this case the distinction is probably necessary for both source parse and target generation. It is certainly indispensable for the correct target generation.

24. EN - *I just arrived*

    ES - *acabo de llegar*

    IT - *sono appena arrivato*

25. EN - *It's just late*

    ES - *es simplemente tarde*

As can be observed, SAL comes in handy, as the distinctions have to do with the different types of adjectives and adverbs. This semantic typology is captured in the SAL language. Therefore, making use of the power of the SAL code, these issues can be resolved.

4.10 Adjective Ordering

When a noun in the source language is modified by more than one adjective, one needs to make decisions on the order these adjectives should follow in the target language. Via TRAN4 rules, the Logos Model encodes ordering restrictions for adjectives. This is not a major issue, but possibly one that creates editing work for translators and is easily solved in target tables.

4.11 Elision in Italian

In Italian, the final vowel of a determiner must be elided in certain contexts. It is handled by the so-called Finish Rules. It is an orthographic pattern which applies to Italian articles and demonstrative adjectives (*uno/una*, *il/lo/la/i/gli/le*, *quello/quella*) when the following word begins with a vowel (e.g., *uno albero* → *un albero*). In certain cases an apostrophe is added (*lo albero* → *l'albero*; *quello albero* → *quell'albero*; *una opera* → *un'opera*; *la opera* → *l'opera*; *quella opera*→ *quell'opera*).

Once the whole translation module has assigned the appropriate transfers and gender settings, Finish Rules will provide the correct spelling adjustments.

4.12 Determiners

A known nightmare in Spanish and Italian generation is the presence or absence of determiners. It seems like an impossible issue to solve at a reasonable cost. Logos does not do well with determiners, but then again, no one does. This is a difficult generation issue to solve and often the approach is to post-edit the incorrect translation rather than generating it.

Logos is a commercial system and, when a development team is deciding what issues to tackle, several factors come into play. Two very important factors for any commercial Generation system are comprehensibility and ease of edition. Generation needs to produce an output that is easily understood (and, of course, faithful to the source), and, if it needs to be edited (often the case with Machine Translation), how easily is the output edited? How many strokes? How many words?, etc.

The case of the determiners in Spanish and Italian is representative of these concerns. For a native speaker it is extremely easy to fix the presence or absence of determiners, and determiners are small words. This explains why a strategy for determiners in Spanish and Italian Generation in the Logos MT system has not been a priority.

5 Conclusions and Future Work

In this paper we have briefly presented Natural Language Generation in its broad sense and the main models and applications that utilize Generation. We have described Generation in the context of the Logos Model. We also provided some examples and raised some relevant questions in the field of Natural Language Generation.

The logical next step in the Logos Model is Target Independent Analysis (TIA). As mentioned earlier, this will allow for modularity and independent linguistic work. But TIA will have to offer an intermediate system where additional source analysis operations might be performed for the sake of the Generation module. Generation needs information to make decisions, and that information must come from somewhere, ideally, from an Interlingua that faithfully and abstractly represents the input. As an example of the consequences of this separation, target SemTab and target verb valence information could be encoded, providing the Generation module with very powerful tools.

From a broad point of view, the Logos Model should probably find a way to integrate statistical and neural models into its rule-based system. Combining the power of these strategies could make the Logos Model the best performing system in the market. Designing and implementing such integration is no easy task, and is beyond the scope of this paper.

References

Anand, Tej andKahn, Gary. 1992. *Making Sense of Gigabytes: A System for Knowledge-Based Market Analysis*. A. C. Nielsen Company. IAAI-92 Proceedings, San Jose, CA, USA.

Arria - http://www.arria.com/science.php

Bach, Nguyen. 2012. *Dependency Structures for Statistical Machine Translation*. Ph.D. Dissertation. Carnegie Mellon University. Pittsburgh, PA, USA

Barreiro, Anabela, Scott, Bernard, Kasper, Walter and Keller, Bernd. 2011. *Open Logos Rule-Based Machine Translation: Philosophy, Model Resources and Customization*. Machine Translation 25, pp 107-126.

Håkan Burden and Rogardt Heldal. 2011. *Natural language generation from class diagrams*. Proceedings of MoDeVVa Proceedings of the 8th International Workshop on Model-Driven Engineering, Verification and Validation. New York, NY, USA

Gdaniec, Claudia. 2002. *Lexical Choice and Syntactic Generation in a Transfer System Transformations in the New LMT English-German System*. In Machine Translation and the Information Soup. Volume 1529 of the series Lecture Notes in Computer Science pp. 408-420.

Lareau, François and Vanner, Leo. 2007. *Towards a Generic Multilingual Dependency Grammar for Text Generation*. Proceedings of the GEAF 2007 Workshop.

Orliac, Brigitte and Dillinger, Mike. 2003. *Collocation extraction for machine translation*. Proceedings of Machine Translation Summit IX: Papers. New Orleans, USA

Phrasomatic - http://www.phrasomatic.net/

Scott, Bernard E. 2018.Translation, Brains and the Computer: A Neurolinguistic Solution to Ambiguity and Complexity in Machine Translation. Machine Translation: Technologies and Applications, vol 2. Springer, Cham.

Scott, Bernard and Barreiro, Anabela. 2009. OpenLogos MT and the SAL representation language. In Proceedings of the First International Workshop on Free/Open-Source Rule-Based Machine Translation, pages 19–26, Alacant, Spain.

Scott, Bernad E. 2003. *The Logos Model: An Historical Perspective*. Machine Translation 18: 1–72. Hingham, MA, USA

Scott, Bernad E. 1992. *Competence, Performance and the Paradigm Shift: a Connectionist Perspective*. Logos Corporation Technology Center, Mount Arlington, NJ.

Scott, Bernard E. 1990. *Biological Neural Net for Parsing Long, Complex Sentences, Logos Corporation Technical Report*. Mount Arlington, NJ, US

Improving Polish to English Neural Machine Translation with Transfer Learning: Effects of Data Volume and Language Similarity

Juuso Eronen
Prefectural University of Kumamoto
eronenj@pu-kumamoto.ac.jp

Michal Ptaszynski
Kitami Institute of Technology
michal@mail.kitami-it.ac.jp

Karol Nowakowski
Tohoku University of Community Service and Science
karol@koeki-u.ac.jp

Zheng Lin Chia
Kitami Institute of Technology
chiazhenglin@gmail.com

Fumito Masui
Kitami Institute of Technology
f-masui@mail.kitami-it.ac.jp

Abstract

This paper investigates the impact of data volume and the use of similar languages on transfer learning in a machine translation task. We find out that having more data generally leads to better performance, as it allows the model to learn more patterns and generalizations from the data. However, related languages can also be particularly effective when there is limited data available for a specific language pair, as the model can leverage the similarities between the languages to improve performance. To demonstrate, we fine-tune mBART model for a Polish-English translation task using the OPUS-100 dataset. We evaluate the performance of the model under various transfer learning configurations, including different transfer source languages and different shot levels for Polish, and report the results. Our experiments show that a combination of related languages and larger amounts of data outperforms the model trained on related languages or larger amounts of data alone. Additionally, we show the importance of related languages in zero-shot and few-shot configurations.

1 Introduction

Machine translation is a vital technology that facilitates communication between people who speak different languages. However, machine translation is a challenging task that requires large amounts of high-quality data for training. Unfortunately, obtaining sufficient data for every language pair can be a difficult and expensive task (Engelson and Dagan, 1996), (Dandapat et al., 2009). Therefore, researchers have turned to transfer learning as a means of improving machine translation performance (Dabre et al., 2020).

The idea of transfer learning is to leverage the knowledge learned from one language pair to improve the performance of a model on another language pair. In most cases, transfer learning is performed from any language with a lot of available data, or by using data from related languages.

Recent research has shown that transfer learning can be an effective approach for improving machine translation performance. It is common to opt to using more data from high-resource languages for a better performance (Zoph et al., 2016). In a study by Kocmi and Bojar (Kocmi and Bojar, 2018), the authors found that the size of the transfer source dataset is more important than the relatedness of the languages. Another way to increase performance with more data is to use multiple source languages for the transfer learning (Maimaiti et al., 2019).

In addition to data quantity, relatedness between languages is also an important factor in transfer learning for machine translation. Related languages share common features, such as grammatical structures and vocabulary, which can be exploited in transfer learning (Nooralahzadeh et al., 2020). In particular, related languages can be effective when there is limited data available for a specific language pair (Cotterell and Heigold, 2017).

In a study by Nguyen and Chiang (Nguyen and Chiang, 2017), the authors investigated the effectiveness of transfer learning using pre-trained models on different language pairs. They found that transfer learning was effective in improving the performance of machine translation models on related language pairs. Similarly, Dabre et al. (Dabre et al., 2017) studied the effectiveness of transfer learning for low-resource languages and found that transfer source languages falling in the same or linguistically similar language family perform the best.

In this paper, we explore the impact of data volume and the use of similar languages in a machine translation task. In practice, we fine-tune the multilingual BART (Tang et al., 2020) model for a Polish to English translation task using the OPUS-100 (Zhang et al., 2020) dataset. We evaluate the performance of the model under different transfer learning configurations, including zero-shot and few-shot configurations. Our study finds that both more data and related languages can be important for transfer learning in machine translation. Having more data can generally lead to better performance, but related languages can be particularly effective when there is limited data available for a specific language pair. Overall, this study contributes to our understanding of the importance of data quantity and language relatedness in transfer learning for machine translation.

2 Previous Research

2.1 Data Volume

Data volume is an important factor in transfer learning for machine translation. Generally, having more data available can lead to better performance. This is because more data provides the model with a larger and more diverse set of examples to learn from, which can lead to improved generalization and better performance on unseen data.

Several studies have shown the effectiveness of increased data quantity for transfer learning in machine translation. For example, in a study by Zoph et al. (Zoph et al., 2016), the authors investigated the effectiveness of using large amounts of data from high-resource languages to improve the performance of machine translation models on low-resource languages. They found that using large amounts of data from high-resource languages can lead to significant improvements in performance on low-resource languages.

Similarly, in a study by Koehn and Knowles (Koehn and Knowles, 2017), the authors investigated the effectiveness of using more data for transfer learning in machine translation across multiple language pairs. They found that using larger amounts of data generally leads to better performance, but the effectiveness of additional data decreases as the amount of data increases.

According to Kocmi and Bojar (Kocmi and Bojar, 2018), the sheer size of the used source corpus can be more important than the relatedness of the source and target languages. They found out that Czech and Estonian sometimes worked better as a language pair than Finnish and Estonian even though the languages are not related.

Also, it has been shown that using multiple languages as the transfer source can lead to higher performance (McDonald et al., 2011). For example, both Maimati et al. (Maimaiti et al., 2019) and Chen et al. (Chen et al., 2019) showed that multi-source cross-lingual transfer can be very effective for machine translation.

2.2 Similar Languages

Relatedness between languages plays an important role in transfer learning for machine translation. Languages that are related or belong to the same language family often share similar grammatical structures, vocabulary, and syntax. This shared linguistic background can be exploited to improve the performance of machine translation systems (Nooralahzadeh et al., 2020).

For example, in a study by Cotterell and Heigold (Cotterell and Heigold, 2017), the authors investigated cross-lingual transfer learning for low-resource languages. They found that related languages, such as Spanish and Portuguese or Czech and Slovak, improved the performance of machine translation models compared to unrelated language pairs.

Relatedness between languages has been found to be an important factor in transfer learning for machine translation. Nguyen and Chiang (Nguyen and Chiang, 2017) found that transfer learning was particularly effective in improving the performance of machine translation models on related language pairs. This is because related languages tend to share common linguistic features, such as grammatical structures and vocabulary, which can be exploited in transfer learning.

Similarly, Dabre et al. (Dabre et al., 2017) found that transfer source languages falling in the same or linguistically similar language family perform the best for low-resource languages. This is because transfer learning can leverage the knowledge learned from the languages to improve the translation quality of the transfer target language.

Relatedness between languages has also been studied in the context of zero-shot and few-shot machine translation, where the goal is to translate between language pairs for which no or very little parallel data is available. Nooralahzadeh et al. (Nooralahzadeh et al., 2020) showed that related languages tend to perform better in zero-shot translation, where the system is trained on a transfer source language and tested on a transfer target language with no parallel data between them.

Relatedness between languages is also important when there is limited data available for a specific language pair. Transfer learning can be particularly effective when there is a lack of parallel data, which is often the case for low-resource languages (Gaikwad et al., 2021). By using related languages, it is possible to leverage existing data and transfer knowledge across languages to improve the performance of machine translation models (Martínez-García et al., 2021).

Additionally, it has been shown that there is a correlation between the similarity of the used language pair and cross-lingual transfer efficiencyfor multiple natural language processing tasks (Lauscher et al., 2020), (Eronen et al., 2023).

3 Methods

In this section, we describe the methodology we used to study the impact of data volume and language similarity on transfer learning in machine translation.

We fine-tuned the multilingual BART (mBART) (Tang et al., 2020) model for the Polish-English translation task. mBART is a pre-trained language model developed by Facebook AI Research (FAIR) that is designed to improve machine translation and other sequence-to-sequence tasks across multiple languages. It is based on the BERT architecture and is trained on a diverse set of languages. mBART has achieved state-of-the-art performance on various machine translation benchmarks and has shown promising results in cross-lingual transfer learning tasks.

The fine-tuning is done using the OPUS-100 corpus. It is a large-scale parallel corpus consisting of more than 100 million sentences in over 100 languages (Zhang et al., 2020). The corpus is designed to facilitate research on multilingual natural language processing, including machine translation, cross-lingual information retrieval, and language modeling. The data is collected from various sources, including web pages, books, and subtitles, and the text is aligned at the sentence level to create parallel corpora for each language pair. Being one of the largest open parallel corpora available, the Opus-100 corpus has become a widely used benchmark dataset for multilingual machine translation and has been used in a number of studies exploring various approaches to multilingual natural language processing.

To evaluate the impact of data volume and the use of related languages, we propose five different models. First, we use a baseline model fine-tuned only on Polish. The other four models are trained in the same manner as Zoph et al.(Zoph et al., 2016) in a parent-child configuration. We fine-tune a parent model first in other languages in a translation task to English. We swap the training corpus and fine-tuning is then continued on these models on the Polish to English task.

The composition of the parent models varies in terms of language similarity, with the first parent model using Czech, a West Slavic language similar to Polish. The second model is fine-tuned in Russian, which is an East Slavic language, a slightly more distant cousin to Polish and Czech. The third model is a Slavic parent model that includes both Czech and Russian, while the fourth model is fine-tuned in German, which is not related to Polish.

To fine-tune the models on the Polish-English task, we use five different configurations. The configurations use different amounts of Polish samples, specifically zero, ten, one hundred, one thousand and ten thousand. Using zero samples means that we evaluate the models in a zero-shot configuration, in which case no Polish data is used for the fine-tuning. By using these different configurations and parent models, we can evaluate the impact of language similarity and data volume on transfer learning in machine translation.

The performance of the machine translation models was evaluated using the BLEU and METEOR metrics. BLEU (Bilingual Evaluation Understudy) is a widely used automatic evaluation metric for machine translation that measures the similarity between the machine-generated translations and the human reference translations (Papineni et al., 2002). The metric ranges from 0 to 1, with higher values indicating better translation quality. The scores are calculated based on the n-gram overlap between the machine-generated and reference translations, as well as the brevity penalty that penalizes the model for generating shorter translations than the reference translations.

METEOR (Metric for Evaluation of Translation with Explicit ORdering) is a widely used evaluation metric in machine translation research, along with BLEU (Banerjee and Lavie, 2005). METEOR is based on a combination of precision, recall, and alignment between the candidate translation and the reference translation, and also considers the fluency and adequacy of the translation. METEOR has been shown to correlate well with human judgments of translation quality and is considered a useful metric for evaluating machine translation performance.

The models were fine-tuned by using PyTorch and the Huggingface Transformers library (Wolf et al., 2020). The hardware used was an Nvidia RTX 3090 GPU.

4 Results and Discussion

We fine-tuned mBART in the configurations introduced earlier. The parent models were fine-tuned using one hundred thousand samples with each of the languages. These models were then additionally fine-tuned with ten thousand, one thousand, one hundred and ten samples of Polish before the evaluation step. The model evaluation scores for all configurations are presented in Table 1.

The table presents the results of the Polish-English translation experiment using different transfer languages at various shot levels of Polish. The experiment was evaluated using the two previously introduced evaluation metrics, BLEU and METEOR. The shot levels represent the amount of Polish data available for fine-tuning the model. The shot levels range from 0 shot (no Polish data) to 10k shot (10,000 samples of Polish used for fine-tuning).

It can be seen from the results that adding higher amounts of transfer target language data (Polish) clearly yield a higher performance. Having more data generally leads to better performance as larger datasets enable the model to learn more patterns and generalizations from the data, which can improve the model's ability to translate accurately. In contradiction to our expectations though, using more transfer source language data does not seem to have so much of an impact. The Slavic model is fine-tuned with twice the amount of data compared to other models as it uses both Czech and Russian data. Despite this, the performance is lower than using only Czech on zero-shot and few-shot cases and lower than using only Russian on more high-resource cases. We need to investigate the use of multiple transfer languages more in the future.

Also, the the results show that related languages are important in zero-shot and few-shot settings, where limited data is available for a given language pair. This has important implications for the development of machine translation models in low-resource scenarios, where transfer learning can be particularly effective. This is because related languages share common features, such as grammatical structures and vocabulary, which can be exploited in transfer learning to improve performance.

This effect seems to diminish however as the amount of transfer target language data (Polish) increases. In more high-resource cases, it does not seem to matter which language is used as the transfer source as with ten thousand samples of Polish, both Russian and German outperform Czech slightly despite Czech being more closely related to Polish than the other languages used. It seems like that with enough samples from the transfer target language, the model can achieve a noticeably higher scores when transferring from any language. Additionally, when the transfer source language is of high similarity (Czech) with source language (Polish), its possible to have completely zero-shot results on comparable or even higher level than in a few-shot configuration with less similar languages (Russian, Slavic).

Our results have implications for the development of machine translation models, particularly for low-resource languages. In such scenarios, related languages may be useful in improving the performance of machine translation models. Fur-

Table 1: BLEU and METEOR scores for Polish-English translation

Source lang: Polish	0 shot		10 shot		100 shot		1k shot		10k shot	
Transfer lang:	BLEU	METEOR	BLEU	METEOR	BLEU	METEOR	BLEU	METEOR	BLEU	METEOR
N/A	–	–	0.45	0.05	0.01	0.01	10.43	0.33	15.42	0.36
Czech	11.61	0.35	14.3	0.41	13.41	0.37	14.35	0.42	17.17	0.41
Russian	0.42	0.11	3.16	0.26	4.86	0.31	16.44	0.41	19.42	0.44
Slavic	8.33	0.27	11.94	0.36	10.87	0.35	16.44	0.41	18.18	0.43
German	0.12	0.05	0.56	0.07	3.72	0.29	16.82	0.42	19.35	0.44

thermore, our findings suggest that efforts to increase the amount of training data available for a given language pair can also lead to improved performance.

One of the main limitations of this study is that we only used one dataset and one language pair, which may limit the generalizability of our findings. The OPUS-100 dataset contains a large amount of data from many languages, but it is still a single dataset and does not fully represent the full range of available content. Similarly, while our study focused on the Polish-English language pair, it is possible that the effectiveness of transfer learning varies across other language pairs.

In the future we are planning to confirm the results with other datasets and other language pairs than Polish-English. We will also investigate the use of related languages in other NLP tasks beyond machine translation, and explore the optimal combination of relatedness and data volume in transfer learning.

Our study suggests that transfer learning can be an effective approach for improving machine translation performance, particularly in low-resource settings. However, further research is needed to investigate the generalizability of our findings to other language pairs and datasets, as well as to explore the effectiveness of transfer learning in more complex real-world settings.

5 Conclusions

In conclusion, our study showed that the volume of the transfer target language data and language similarity can have a significant impact on transfer learning in machine translation. Contrary to our expectations, using additional transfer source language data did not seem to make a difference. The results indicate that having more data generally leads to better performance, but related languages can be particularly effective when there is limited data available for a specific language pair. Our experiments with different parent models and fine-tuning configurations demonstrate that incorporating language similarity in transfer learning can help improve machine translation performance, especially in low-resource scenarios.

Based on our results, we recommend that researchers and practitioners consider language similarity when designing transfer learning approaches for machine translation. When there is limited data available for a specific language pair, incorporating related languages in the training data can improve performance.

In the future, we need to confirm the results also with other datasets and other language pairs. We need to investigate the use of related languages in other NLP tasks beyond machine translation, and explore the the use of multiple transfer source languages more in the future.

Overall, our study contributes to a better understanding of the factors that influence transfer learning in machine translation and provides insights into how to design effective transfer learning approaches for this task. We hope that our findings will be useful for researchers and practitioners working in the field of natural language processing and machine translation.

References

Banerjee, Satanjeev and Alon Lavie. 2005. METEOR: An automatic metric for MT evaluation with improved correlation with human judgments. In *Proceedings of the ACL Workshop on Intrinsic and Extrinsic Evaluation Measures for Machine Translation and/or Summarization*, pages 65–72, Ann Arbor, Michigan, June. Association for Computational Linguistics.

Chen, Xilun, Ahmed Hassan Awadallah, Hany Hassan, Wei Wang, and Claire Cardie. 2019. Multi-source cross-lingual model transfer: Learning what to share. In *Proceedings of the 57th Annual Meeting of the Association for Computational Linguistics*, pages 3098–3112, Florence, Italy, July. Association for Computational Linguistics.

Cotterell, Ryan and Georg Heigold. 2017. Cross-lingual character-level neural morphological tagging. In *Proceedings of the 2017 Conference on Empirical Methods in Natural Language Processing*, pages 748–759, Copenhagen, Denmark, September. Association for Computational Linguistics.

Dabre, Raj, Tetsuji Nakagawa, and Hideto Kazawa. 2017. An empirical study of language relatedness for transfer learning in neural machine translation. In *Pacific Asia Conference on Language, Information and Computation*.

Dabre, Raj, Chenhui Chu, and Anoop Kunchukuttan. 2020. A survey of multilingual neural machine translation. *ACM Comput. Surv.*, 53(5), September.

Dandapat, Sandipan, Priyanka Biswas, Monojit Choudhury, and Kalika Bali. 2009. Complex linguistic annotation–no easy way out! a case from bangla and hindi pos labeling tasks. In *Proceedings of the Third Linguistic Annotation Workshop (LAW III)*, pages 10–18.

Engelson, Sean P. and Ido Dagan. 1996. Minimizing manual annotation cost in supervised training from corpora. In *Proceedings of the 34th Annual Meeting on Association for Computational Linguistics*, ACL '96, page 319–326, USA. Association for Computational Linguistics.

Eronen, Juuso, Michal Ptaszynski, and Fumito Masui. 2023. Zero-shot cross-lingual transfer language selection using linguistic similarity. *Information Processing & Management*, 60(3):103250.

Gaikwad, Saurabh, Tharindu Ranasinghe, Marcos Zampieri, and Christopher M. Homan. 2021. Cross-lingual offensive language identification for low resource languages: The case of marathi.

Kocmi, Tom and Ondřej Bojar. 2018. Trivial transfer learning for low-resource neural machine translation. In *Proceedings of the Third Conference on Machine Translation: Research Papers*, pages 244–252, Brussels, Belgium, October. Association for Computational Linguistics.

Koehn, Philipp and Rebecca Knowles. 2017. Six challenges for neural machine translation. In *Proceedings of the First Workshop on Neural Machine Translation*, pages 28–39, Vancouver, August. Association for Computational Linguistics.

Lauscher, Anne, Vinit Ravishankar, Ivan Vulić, and Goran Glavaš. 2020. From zero to hero: On the limitations of zero-shot language transfer with multilingual Transformers. In *Proceedings of the 2020 Conference on Empirical Methods in Natural Language Processing (EMNLP)*, pages 4483–4499, Online, November. Association for Computational Linguistics.

Maimaiti, M., Yang Liu, Huanbo Luan, and Maosong Sun. 2019. Multi-round transfer learning for low-resource nmt using multiple high-resource languages. *ACM Transactions on Asian and Low-Resource Language Information Processing (TALLIP)*, 18:1 – 26.

Martínez-García, Antonio, Toni Badia, and Jeremy Barnes. 2021. Evaluating morphological typology in zero-shot cross-lingual transfer. In *Proceedings of the 59th Annual Meeting of the Association for Computational Linguistics and the 11th International Joint Conference on Natural Language Processing (Volume 1: Long Papers)*, pages 3136–3153, Online, August. Association for Computational Linguistics.

McDonald, Ryan, Slav Petrov, and Keith Hall. 2011. Multi-source transfer of delexicalized dependency parsers. In *Proceedings of the Conference on Empirical Methods in Natural Language Processing*, EMNLP '11, page 62–72, USA. Association for Computational Linguistics.

Nguyen, Toan Q. and David Chiang. 2017. Transfer learning across low-resource, related languages for neural machine translation. In *International Joint Conference on Natural Language Processing*.

Nooralahzadeh, Farhad, Giannis Bekoulis, Johannes Bjerva, and Isabelle Augenstein. 2020. Zero-shot cross-lingual transfer with meta learning. In *Proceedings of the 2020 Conference on Empirical Methods in Natural Language Processing (EMNLP)*, pages 4547–4562, Online, November. Association for Computational Linguistics.

Papineni, Kishore, Salim Roukos, Todd Ward, and Wei-Jing Zhu. 2002. Bleu: a method for automatic evaluation of machine translation. In *Proceedings of the 40th Annual Meeting of the Association for Computational Linguistics*, pages 311–318, Philadelphia, Pennsylvania, USA, July. Association for Computational Linguistics.

Tang, Yuqing, Chau Tran, Xian Li, Peng-Jen Chen, Naman Goyal, Vishrav Chaudhary, Jiatao Gu, and Angela Fan. 2020. Multilingual translation with extensible multilingual pretraining and finetuning.

Wolf, Thomas, Lysandre Debut, Victor Sanh, Julien Chaumond, Clement Delangue, Anthony Moi, Pierric Cistac, Tim Rault, Remi Louf, Morgan Funtowicz, Joe Davison, Sam Shleifer, Patrick von Platen, Clara Ma, Yacine Jernite, Julien Plu, Canwen Xu, Teven Le Scao, Sylvain Gugger, Mariama Drame, Quentin Lhoest, and Alexander Rush. 2020. Transformers: State-of-the-art natural language processing. In *Proceedings of the 2020 Conference on Empirical Methods in Natural Language Processing: System Demonstrations*, pages 38–45, Online, October. Association for Computational Linguistics.

Zhang, Biao, Philip Williams, Ivan Titov, and Rico Sennrich. 2020. Improving massively multilingual neural machine translation and zero-shot translation. In

Proceedings of the 58th Annual Meeting of the Association for Computational Linguistics, pages 1628–1639, Online, July. Association for Computational Linguistics.

Zoph, Barret, Deniz Yuret, Jonathan May, and Kevin Knight. 2016. Transfer learning for low-resource neural machine translation. In *Conference on Empirical Methods in Natural Language Processing*.

A Multilingual Paraphrasary of Multiwords

Anabela Barreiro
INESC-ID
Rua Alves Redol, 9
1000-029 Lisboa, Portugal
anabela.barreiro@inesc-id.pt

Cristina Mota
INESC-ID
Rua Alves Redol, 9
1000-029 Lisboa, Portugal
cristina.mota@inesc-id.pt

Abstract

This paper introduces the novel concept of a Multilingual Paraphrasary addressing its need for paraphrasing and translation. The multilingual paraphrasary is an ongoing work carried out in compliance with the CLUE-Alignments, a set of linguistically informed multilingual alignments, comprising several categories of multiword units. The CLUE-Alignments set has all possible combinations between English, French, Portuguese, and Spanish parallel texts of the common test set of the Europarl corpus. The gold collection of the manually annotated CLUE-Alignments is a refined Gold-CLUE. The paper also presents the CLUE-Aligner tool[1], developed to facilitate the alignment of the meaning and translation units in the bitexts, including the alignment of non-contiguous units. Our approach benefits from the Logos Model for machine translation, namely the semantico-syntactic abstraction language SAL and the semantic table SemTab. Finally, the paper illustrates how the collected paraphrases are used in the paraphrase generation tool eSPERTo[2], developed for Portuguese, as part of a larger multilingual generation project involving paraphrasing and translation.

[1]https://esperto.hlt.inesc-id.pt/esperto/aligner/index.pl

[2]https://esperto.hlt.inesc-id.pt/esperto/esperto/demo.pl

1 Introduction

Paraphrase generation is crucial in natural language processing (NLP) and quality machine translation (MT) cannot be achieved without comparable quality paraphrase knowledge because paraphrases are vital to deploying semantic knowledge to guarantee high fidelity translation. An important common issue in human translation and MT is to define equivalence and to define and establish paraphrasing capabilities. Therefore, one of the first tasks involved in the construction of a paraphrasing or MT system should be to collect pairs of alignments that correspond to semantically identical or similar units of meaning expressed with different vocabulary and/or syntactic structure. Some paraphrase extraction techniques may simply imply semi-automatic procedures, while others may consist of supervised alignment trained on manual alignments, which can be used for monolingual or bilingual term extraction.

We used the common test version of the European Parliament Proceedings taken from Q4/2000 portion of the data, 2000-10 to 2000-12 (Koehn, 2005). The bilingual texts are available on the European Parliament Proceedings Parallel Corpus website.[3] The reference sub-corpus is aligned at the sentence level, ranging from sentence number 101 to sentence number 500. Our work represents an extension of the work on multilingual alignments by (Graça et al., 2008). We manually annotated translation alignments for 400 sentences in 6 sets of the multilingual test corpus, representing 2,400 aligned sentences.

Our research led to the identification of four main classes of challenges to the alignment of

[3]http://www.statmt.org/europarl/archives.html#v1

units: (i) lexical and semantico-syntactic, (ii) morphological, (iii) morpho-syntactic, and (iv) semantico-discursive). Our focus is on the lexical and semantico-syntactic phenomena that MT systems, in general, do not translate well, namely the alignment of multilingual/cross-lingual expressions, multiwords, and other phrasal units as representation objects in the alignment between the source and target languages. In order to simplify the wording, we will use the designation of multiwords for the three types of semantico-syntactic translation units aforementioned.[4] The alignment task resulted in a paraphrase collection to be used in NLP applications including MT. We analysed the collection and created a novel linguistic computational object/concept, which we coined 'Paraphrasary', as a complex equivalent to a dictionary at a level larger than the word. A paraphrasary is to semantico-syntactic units' equivalences as a dictionary is to synonyms.

The structure of the remainder of the paper is as follows: in Section 2, we revisit the research on alignments, revise the concept of alignment, and justify our need for linguistic precision in the alignment task. In Section 3, we discuss the complexity of the alignment of multiwords. In Section 4, we explain how the Logos Model approach to the processing of units of meaning larger than the word (multiwords) helped configure our alignment model. In Section 5, we present the **C**ross-**L**ingual **U**nit **E**licitation (CLUE) approach, summarise the CLUE-Aligner tool and the gold collection Gold-CLUE. In Section 6, we describe how we choose what goes into the multilingual Paraphrasary. In Section 7, we illustrate how the collected paraphrases are used in the eSPERTo paraphrase generation system. Finally, in Section 8, we present some conclusions and future work.

2 Alignments Revisited

Word alignments were defined as representations of semantically equivalent words, phrases, or expressions within the source and target sentences of a parallel corpus (Brown et al., 1990), and the task of word alignment consists of identifying the translational equivalences that contain semantic correspondences in the aligned sentence pairs of a parallel text (Hearne and Way, 2011). As the outcome of the alignment task, a set of individual alignments or links, as some authors call them (Lambert et al., 2005), can be established between words or sequences of words, designated as n-grams. A sequence of more than one n-gram is usually called 'phrase'. Alignments based on random n-grams do not have a linguistic motivation or contrastive analysis lying behind them. However, MT systems built upon linguistic knowledge-based alignments extracted from high-quality translation corpora can contribute to increased precision, with the subsequent improvement of translation quality. Additional benefits can be gained for any natural language generation (NLG) task because "word alignments" is not a concept restricted to MT. They are used in a wide variety of applications, representing a highly valuable resource for evaluation and enhancement of word alignment algorithms, supervised word alignment, alignment evaluation, MT evaluation, automatic bilingual lexica, term extraction, and paraphrasing.[5]

Shortcomings in alignment tasks and alignment guidelines show that linguistic expertise and cross-lingual contrastive analysis are required to reduce the complexity and ambiguity in the alignment process, especially with regard to multiwords because linguistic principles can support alignment decisions independently of the annotator or the annotator's perception of what a translational equivalence should be. The paper "n-grams in search of theories" (Maia et al., 2008) claimed the need to create linguistically robust alignment tools for research based on a supporting theoretical and practical framework. As a follow up, the development of CLUE-Aligner[6] (Barreiro et al., 2016) appeared as a response to the demand for the alignment of not only contiguous multiwords, such as the support verb construction *to draw a distinction between* but also non-contiguous multiwords, i.e., units with insertions, such as the support verb construction *to bring* [INSERTION] *to a conclusion* (Barreiro and Batista, 2016). Our alignment task led to the development of a set of guidelines – CLUE-Alignments –

[4]Alignments are an efficient (and convenient) intermediate representation developed for engineering purposes in NLP and MT systems that present shortcomings from a linguistic point-of-view. We are trying to reduce the number of shortcomings in alignment tasks by adding scientific precision.

[5]Some basic annotation guidelines had been proposed, e.g. http://www.cs.jhu.edu/~ccb/publications/paraphrase_guidelines.pdf

[6]CLUE-Aligner is an alignment tool based on Linear-B (Callison-Burch and Bannard, 2004), enhanced in order to permit the alignment and storage of both contiguous and non-contiguous multiwords and other phrasal units to be used in paraphrasing and translation.

based on the fundamental principles of the Logos Machine Translation Model (henceforth, the Logos Model) (Scott, 2003) (Barreiro et al., 2011)[7], which relies on deep semantico-syntactic analysis to generate translation of multiwords, such as in the English-Portuguese (EN-PT) examples: (i) *give in without struggle — ceder sem resistência*; (ii) NHum/PRO *be settling down to* PRO *new job* — NHum/PRO *ir-se habituando ao novo emprego*; or (iii) *arrive first/second/last — chegar em primeiro/segundo/último lugar*. Quality texts and quality alignments based on the "SemTab" function of the Logos Model (Section 4) were key ingredients to build an efficient multilingual paraphrasary, which represents a step forward into meaningful quality translation, and a valuable resource for NLG. Section 3 discusses the challenges presented by multiwords to MT and the reasons why their correct and non-ambiguous alignment is important.

3 Multiwords

Multiwords, most commonly known as multiword expressions[8], have been defined by (Baldwin and Kim, 2010) as "lexical items that: (a) can be decomposed into multiple lexemes; and (b) display lexical, syntactic, semantic, pragmatic, and/or statistical idiomaticity". The specification of several classes of multiwords reflects some progress in their classification. Literature draws attention to different types of multiwords: phrasal verbs, light or support verb constructions, noun compounds, proper names, and non-compositional idioms, among others. Nevertheless, the struggles of MT with multiwords are known and have been reported in several research works (Barreiro et al., 2010), (Barreiro et al., 2013), (Kordoni and Simova, 2014), (Barreiro et al., 2014), and (Barreiro, 2015), among others.

Multiwords are a source of mistranslations not only by MT systems, but also by professional translators, in part because they can be non-contiguous and the remote syntactic dependency may get lost or misunderstood, but also because they are a source of various **contextual nuances**, such as the prepositional verb *break into* in the EN-PT alignment pairs: (i) *break into* NPlace — *assaltar* NPlace as in *beak into a house — assaltar uma casa*; (ii) *break into a laugh — desatar a rir*; (iii) *break into a run — pôr-se em fuga, pôr-se a andar*; but (iv) *break into pieces — quebrar em bocados, estrilhaçar*.

The most important consideration with respect to multiwords is that they should never be processed on a word-for-word basis because they represent atomic semantico-syntactic and translation units and cannot be broken down into constituent parts in any alignment process.

Therefore, linguistic knowledge "elicited" in the alignment process and the use of a more refined alignment tool can solve some of the problems related to multiword alignment when it is so relevant that these alignments mirror the unity of the expression, a challenge that was addressed successfully in the Logos Model, as demonstrated next.

4 The Logos Model Approach

The Logos Model has been described with a great degree of detail in (Scott, 2003), (Scott and Barreiro, 2009), and (Scott, 2018), among others. We highlight in this paper only the SAL language and the SemTab function for the sake of illustrating how relevant they are for our approach to the processing and generation of multiwords and the establishment of bilingual and multilingual paraphrasaries.

4.1 Semantico-Syntactic Abstraction Language (SAL)

In the Logos Model, natural language is represented as a refined Semantico-Syntactic Abstraction Language (SAL), also designated as a hierarchical ontology, with categories for all parts of speech. When processing the sentence, word strings are converted into SAL patterns. SAL has four levels of abstraction: (i) a syntactic level (word class) and three levels referred to as (ii) superset, (iii) set, and (iv) subset. Figure 1 illustrates the hierarchical structure for the SAL Superset Animate-type nouns, where the Sets are in red and the Subsets are in blue. It is possible to apply the same techniques to the data, which in the Logos Model are not literal words, but SAL entities or SAL patterns. This is the reason why it makes sense to train machine learning (ML) systems to learn new SAL patterns based on alignments, instead of on the conventionally-used MT patterns.

[7]The Logos Model underlies both the commercial system and its open source version OpenLogos.

[8]This term has also been designated *inter alia* as "multiword lexical items", "phraseological units" and "fixed expressions", with slight variations in scope and meaning.

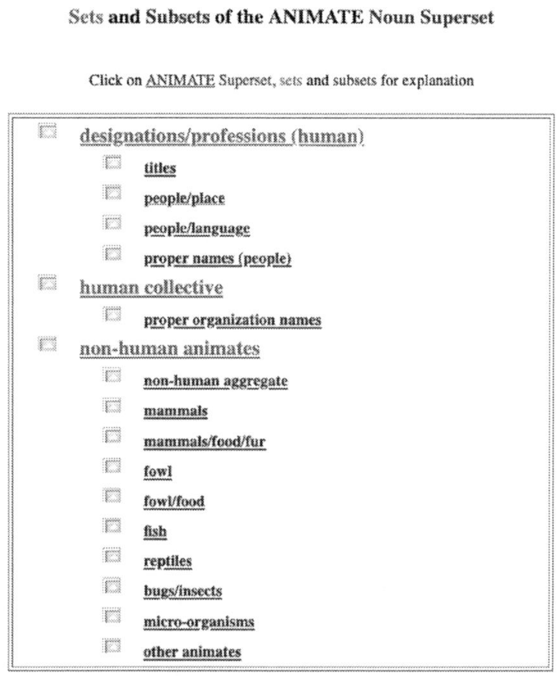

Figure 1: SAL Superset Animate-type Nouns

The objects of alignment provide a multilingual dictionary-type function, which we call **Paraphrasary**, that clarifies, simplifies, and adds precision to text, and to its translation (cf. Section 6).

4.2 The Sematic Table (SemTab)

In the Logos Model, all multiwords are represented as rules in a separate database, the Semantic Table or "SemTab", as described in (Orliac and Dillinger, 2003). In our alignment research work, we propose a methodological framework for the alignment task that relies on the use of multiwords as representation objects of alignment. The meaning is derived from the semantic processing in the SemTab function, where multiwords can be linguistically processed and translation fidelity can be improved. For example, SemTab allows distinguishing between the multiword (i) *be acquainted with* N(AN-Hum)/PRO — *conhecer* N/PRO *pessoalmente*, where the translation of the verb depends on the type of noun (human-type) and the multiword (ii) *be acquainted with* N-Abs — *estar ao corrente de* N-Abs, where the noun N is abstract (Abs) of the type "Information", e.g., a piece of news, a gossip, situation, etc. On the other hand, from the sentence (iii) *he was driving the car at full speed*, the noun *car* can be replaced by any type of concrete, vehicle: *drive* N(CO-Vehic) *at full speed* — *guiar/conduzir* N(CO-Vehic) *a toda a velocidade*. In the Logos Model, SemTab rules deploy SAL patterns or entities, such as the aforementioned N(AN-Hum), N(Abs-info-type), or N(CO-Vehic).

In the Europarl corpus, not all translations are optimal and often translational equivalents are approximate rather than exact. In example (1), the English prepositional verb *to deal with* is translated in the Romance languages as *dedicarse a* (*engage in*) in Spanish, the reflexive *s'attacher à* (*focus on/stick to*) in French, and *centrar-se em* (*concentrate/center/focus on*) in Portuguese.

(1) *EN* - our Asian partners prefer **to deal with** questions which unite us

ES - nuestros socios asiáticos prefieren **dedicarse a** las questiones que nos unen

FR - nos partenaires asiatiques préfèrent **s'attacher à** ([**a**+a]) ce qui nous unit

PT - os nossos parceiros asiáticos preferem **centrar-se** unicamente **n**as ([**em**+as]) questões comuns

The Logos Model allows for the application of a SemTab contextual rule, such as the one in Example 2, which is a deep structure pattern that matches on/applies to a great variety of surface structures.

(2) DEAL(VI) WITH N(questions) = S'OCCUPER DE N[9]

The differences in the translations of *deal* are related to the idiomatic ways that predicate nouns select their support verbs in different languages: *take a vow* in English, but "*make a vow*" in the Romance languages (*hacer* in Spanish, *faire* in French, and *fazer* in Portuguese). Verbal expressions such as the English prepositional verb *to deal with* take different senses (and translations) depending on contexts, typically their object or prepositional phrase complement. If the context of the verb is *to deal with questions*, as in (1), then the French translation should be *s'occuper de* (*to be busy with*). On the other hand, if the context is *he proved unable to deal with the problem*, then the translation should be the translation of its paraphrase *handle the problem*. However, if the context is *he refused to deal with the problem*, then the translation would be a translation of the paraphrase *analyse and try to solve the problem*. These different nuances are related to the ambiguity and

[9]Here we only display the comment line of the SemTab rule, not the rule itself or what it does in terms of the Logos language. The rule notation is arcane due to its numeric representation and it would take a larger effort to explain the use and meaning of the distinct codes in the Logos Model.

weakness of the verb *deal* and the different meanings of the predicate-like nouns *questions* (*issues*, *topics*, *interrogations*, etc.) or *problem* (*difficulty*, *exercise*, etc.). It is the meaning of these nouns that triggers the different translations of *deal*, just like the verb *take* will have different translations depending on the predicate noun it supports (*walk*, *responsibility*, *comfort*, etc.). Therefore, the two slightly different meanings for *problem* in the last two examples explain the distinct paraphrase: *handle*, in one case, and *analyse and try to solve*, in the other case. In the exemplified context, the SemTab rule states that when followed by the direct object noun *questions* or a noun with the same semantico-syntactic information, the verb is translated as *s'occuper de*, overriding the default dictionary translation of this verb. The power and advantage of the rule in the Logos Model with regard to non-contiguous multiwords is the ability of the MT system to recognise, analyse, and relate constituents that are apart (even far apart) in the sentence.

Former word alignment techniques, even when they contemplated multiword alignments, were unable to present a consistent and efficient solution to process non-contiguous expressions. In other words, SemTab is an effective way of analysing and translating words in context, especially when the context is remote.

In addition to the long-distance dependency capability, SemTab also allows generalising between alternative forms of the same multiword. For example, it presents the possibility of generalising translations of *take a walk* to translations of *walk*, if one of these two is found in the training corpus. Similarly, closed class items or highly frequent multiwords might be learned quickly and be translated correctly by state-of-the-art MT systems, but open class items or less frequent multiwords might present more challenging problems that can be observed in MT output, but also in non-native speakerisms, such as the choice of a support verb for a particular support verb construction (e.g., *make a visit to* N or *pay a visit to* N, which can be robustly corrected by the use of SemTab.

5 CLUE – Cross-Lingual Unit Elicitation

Under the umbrella of CLUE, we developed a set of alignment guidelines, an alignment tool, and a gold collection. For the alignment task, we used the bilingual corpora from the Europarl corpus.

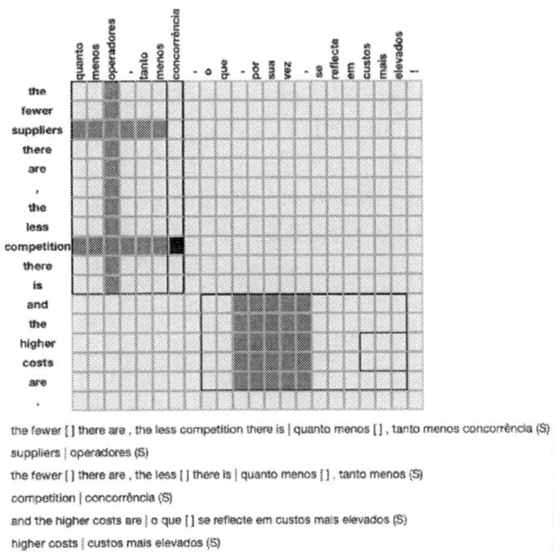

Figure 2: Alignment of comparison and metonymy *the fewer* [] *there are*, [] *the less* [] *there is* — *quanto menos* [], *tanto menos*

The Gold-CLUE was facilitated by the use of the CLUE-Aligner alignment tool. Both the Guidelines and the Gold-CLUE require revision and refinement. So far, the only revised Gold-CLUE was for the EN-PT language pair.

5.1 CLUE-Aligner

CLUE-Aligner is an alignment tool developed to annotate paraphrasing or translation units representing multiwords found in monolingual or bilingual pairs of parallel sentences (Barreiro et al., 2016). CLUE-Aligner is based on another alignment tool, Linear-B (Callison-Burch and Bannard, 2004), but it was extended in order to allow the alignment of contiguous and non-contiguous multiwords, addressing the long-distance dependency that characterises the majority of semantico-syntactic patterns.

CLUE-Aligner allows the loading of previously generated alignments (segments) for the corpora parallel sentences. During the annotation task, the annotator manually corrects any inaccurate alignments (either gathered manually or automatically), and defines the new alignments for multiwords, which represent translation (or paraphrasing) units.

Figure 2 illustrates the alignment of the non-contiguous comparison/metonymy *the fewer* [] *there are*, [] *the less* [] *there is* — *quanto menos* [], *tanto menos*, and *the higher* [] *are* — *o que se reflecte em* [] *mais elevados*. In this figure of speech, the insertions were excluded and aligned independently: *suppliers* was aligned with *operadores*, *competition* was aligned with *concorrência*, and *costs* — was aligned with *custos*. On the CLUE-Aligner interface, in Figure 2, the linguistic annotator can immediately see the list of alignments in text format and correct any error that might have been done in the alignment task.

5.2 Gold-CLUE

The Gold-CLUE is the gold collection made of aligned multiwords resultant from our alignment task. The Gold-CLUE contemplates a set of linguistic phenomena that can be classified into four main classes: (1) lexical and semantico-syntactic challenges include multiwords, such as support verb constructions, compound/modal verbs, and prepositional predicates; (2) morphological challenges include contracted forms, lexical versus non-lexical realisation, that is, lexical items that are present in one language but not the other, such as determiners (articles and zero/missing articles), and pro-drop phenomena including subject pronoun dropping, and empty relative pronouns; (3) morpho-syntactic challenges include free noun adjuncts (noun-noun compounds); and (4) semantico-discursive challenges include emphatic linguistic constructions, such as pleonasm and tautology, repetition, and focus constructions. For lack of space in this paper to exemplify and discuss the most problematic alignment problems, and justify the annotation decisions for all the classes identified, we restrict our exemplification to class (1), specifically with support verb constructions' phenomena.

5.2.1 Support Verb Constructions

A support verb construction is a multiword or complex predicate consisting of a semantically weak verb (the support verb), and a predicate noun, a predicate adjective, or, much less frequently, a predicate adverb (*make a presentation*, *make it simple* or *go fast*) (Barreiro, 2009).[10] In the Europarl corpus, support verb constructions are either aligned with semantically equivalent single verbs (many-to-one correspondence) or with other semantically equivalent support verb constructions (many-to-many correspondence). For example, the English, French, and Portuguese prepositional transitive support verb constructions *draw a distinction (between)*, *faire une distinction (entre)*, and *estabelecer uma diferença (entre)*, align with the Spanish prepositional transitive verb *distinguir (entre)* (*distinguish (between)*), as illustrated in Example (3). English and Portuguese use non-elementary support verbs *draw* and *estabelecer* (*establish*), while French uses an elementary support verb *faire* (*make*). Smaller alignments can be established between the intransitive support verb constructions *draw a distinction*, *faire une distinction*, and *estabelecer uma diferença* and the Spanish verb *distinguir*.These alignments would be necessary to translate the support verb construction when it is used intransitively.

(3) EN - we need **to draw a distinction between** north and south

ES - debemos **distinguir entre** norte y sur

FR - nous devons **faire une distinction entre** le nord et sud

PT - temos de **estabelecer uma diferença entre** norte e sul

5.2.2 Alignment Decisions

The Europarl corpus subset that we used contains several instances of non-contiguous support verb constructions. In translation, a non-contiguous expression in a source language can be maintained in the target language or replaced by an equivalent but contiguous expression that conveys the same meaning. It can also be transformed into a simpler contiguous syntactic structure, such as a single word.[11] In example (4), the non-contiguous English support verb construction *set in motion*, corresponding to the Portuguese equivalent single verb *empreender* (*undertake*), is used instead of maintaining the English structure, with a support verb construction to express a similar meaning. Both Spanish and French maintain the support verb construction (*llevar a cabo* and *mettre en chantier*), with the difference that in these languages the support verb constructions are contiguous and have no insertions. The existence of a non-contiguous expression in one of the sentences of the language pair causes additional complexity to the alignment task, which we are able to solve with the Logos approach.

[10]For a broader definition of support verb and support verb construction, see also (Jespersen, 1965), (Erbach and Krenn, 1993), and (Butt, 2010), among others.

[11]In some cases, the verbal expression is always expressed in the form of a support verb construction (cf. non-elementary support verb construction *play* [INSERTION] *role*) because there is no suitable corresponding single verb, which is semantically equivalent to the support verb construction (Barreiro, 2009).

(4) $_{EN}$ - many member states thus have the major task of **setting** structural reform **in motion**

$_{ES}$ - he aquí por lo tanto una tarea de gran importancia para que numerosos estados miembros **lleven a cabo** reformas estructurales

$_{FR}$ - il y a donc là une táche considérable pour beaucoup d'états membres, celle de **mettre en chantier** des réformes structurelles

$_{PT}$ - há, portanto, uma tarefa importante para muitos estados-membros em **empreender** reformas estruturais

To sum up, non-contiguous support verb constructions processing, recognition, and translation is a challenging problem when using alignment techniques and some previous methodologies violate the intrinsic property of the unit as an atomic group of elements when aligning them individually or when not respecting the correct boundaries of the unit. However, inspired by the Logos Model, we came up with a way of aligning them successfully in CLUE-Aligner. CLUE-Guidelines propose that individual word alignments should not be annotated inside the support verb construction block. There is no linguistic motivation to align the canonical form of the support verb and do a separate alignment for the optional and variable parts of the construction. However, when inserted constituents are equivalent in the source and target languages, these constituents are aligned as separate elements, outside the multiword unit.

Among several other somehow arbitrary decisions, we have not addressed whether the alignment of non-contiguous support verb constructions with pronominal insertions should be aligned. Would it be pragmatically justified the alignment of, for example, the expression *setting* PRON-*it in motion*? Probably, yes. Although, from a practical point of view, the alignment of this phrase can be justified, it needs to be tested what is pragmatically more adequate for a particular application, the inclusion of insertions or no inclusion of insertions of each grammatical category. For example, the alignment of pronominal elements, where there is a pronoun in the source language and a lexical element in the target language (or vice-versa), may be correct from a point of view of a text that needs to be analysed contrastively, but this does not teach correctly an MT system, and therefore, should be left out of the training data. On the other hand, the alignments where both source and target languages contain equivalent pronominal alignments, represent good training data. With regard to adverbs, they are free modifiers and normally less polysemous and less ambiguous than nouns, verbs, and adjectives, which makes the task easier for humans and machines. The alignment of insertions in a non-contiguous multiword unit needs to be further discussed for each particular application, due to considerations related to the word order of the insertions for each language, among others.

5.2.3 Methodology

In order to achieve a provisional first round of results, a polyglot linguist, with knowledge of the four languages covered in this study, annotated manually the total of 2,400 sentence alignments (400 x 6 language pairs) and built the CLUE-Guidelines based on linguistic knowledge as processed in the Logos Model, paying special attention to multiwords and other translation units. From the dataset of 400 sentences of the corpus, for the EN-PT language pair, a total of 3,700 multiword alignments were collected. They all represent candidates for entries in our Paraphrasary. Table 1 shows some examples.

Sentence Pair #	English– Portuguese
4	have [ ] margin for discretion ter [ ] margem de discricionalidade
181	between [ ] and [ ] million people entre [ ] e [ ] milhões de pessoas
207	have not [ ] been in favour of não se mostraram favoráveis a
237	would [ ] mainly focus on visa
279	cross - border services serviços além fronteiras
307	before [ ] even antes ainda de
308	what must underpin que deve subjazer a
316	avenues which could be explored pistas a seguir

Table 1: EN-PT Alignments

6 Multilingual Paraphrasary

Our research on paraphrasing applications shows that both monolingual and multilingual paraphrase generation require the development of paraphrasaries. Paraphrasary is a new concept of organising linguistic data in a repository (or several repositories), which can grow into a large body of paraphrastic knowledge. It is a database of multiword entries listed alphabetically validated by a linguist after these multiwords have been aligned during the alignment task. For example, the alignment 181 in Table 1, *between* [ ] *and* [ ] *million people — entre* [ ] *e* [ ] *milhões de pessoas*, can enter the Paraphrasary via a SemTab-type rule that allows generating a large number of instances. Example (5) shows how the alignment can become much broader by using some constraints, such as [Num], a numeric expression.

(5) between [NUM] and [NUM] N = entre [NUM] e [NUM] de N

Via the power of generalisation that SAL categories allow, an alignment pair gathered from the corpus can be used in the generation of thousands of multilingual paraphrases. The development of paraphrasaries is, therefore, the kick-start of a paraphrasing tool.

7 eSPERTo Paraphrasing System

The eSPERTo paraphrasing system is an online platform[12] that allows rewriting different kinds of expressions using the NooJ linguistic engine (Silberztein, 2015; Silberztein, 2003). (Barreiro et al., 2022) present an overview of the system and lexicon-grammar resources that allow for the easy paraphrasing of constructions involving human intransitive adjectives, and also predicate nouns with support verbs *fazer* (do) and *ser de* (be of).

In Figure 3, we illustrate a simple example of using the multilingual paraphrasary to translate multiwords of a sentence in Portuguese into different paraphrases in English. eSPERTo uses grammars that identify multiwords in a source language, such as *constitui uma provocação* (literally, *it constitutes a provocation*) in Portuguese. When clicking on this multiword, the text changes to green and the translations of the multiword appear in a drop-down list. For the Portuguese multiword, eSPERTo shows 3 paraphrases in English: *is provoking*; *it is a public outrage*; and *is provocative*. The suggested translations were paraphrasing pairs in Gold-CLUE and entries in the (EN-PT) Paraphrasary where the same multiword in Portuguese were translations of different multiwords in English. Therefore, as illustrated in Figure 4, the multiword in Portuguese is represented as input of the graph by its constituents: `<constituir,V>` will match any form of the ver *constituir* in the text, and `<N+EN>` will match *provocação*, which will be stored in the variable `$Npred`. Then, the top path of the graph will output *it is a public outrage* whereas the bottom path will output the translation of *provocação* stored in the variable `$Npred` - `$Npred$EN` - preceded by *is*.

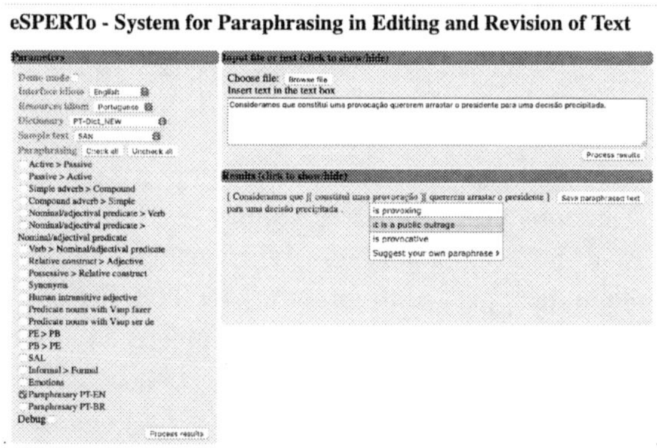

Figure 3: Translating Portuguese expression to English paraphrases in eSPERTo

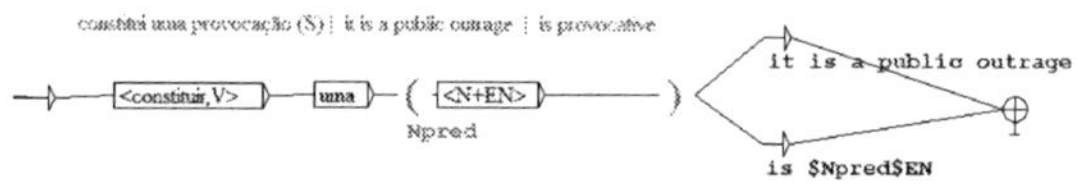

Figure 4: Paraphrasary grammar: *constituir uma provocação*

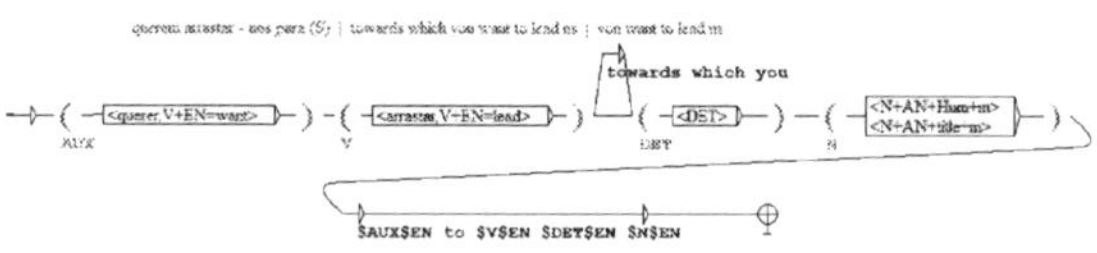

Figure 5: Paraphrasary grammar: *arrastar* [N+AN+Hum] *para*

In Figure 5, we illustrate the simplified paraphrasary grammar that allowed for the generation of the distinct translations into English of the multiword [`QUERER`] `arrastar` [`NP+AN+HUM`]. Each multiword constituent will be stored in different variables (`$AUX`, `$V`, `$DET`, and `$N`) in order to use them to translate them (respectively, `$AUX$EN`, `$V$EN`, `$DET$EN`, and `$N$EN`)). This grammar uses the SAL codes `+AN`, `+hum`, and `+title` to restrict the noun in the noun phrase to be human-type.

These grammars take advantage of the multilingual nature of NooJ and other properties included in the dictionary entries, but the full integration of the paraphrasary into the eSPERTo system is still under progress as it is not yet clear what is the best way of tackling this integration.

[12]eSPERTo stands for 'System for Paraphrasing in Editing and Revision of Text'. The system can be tested at: https://esperto.hlt.inesc-id.pt/esperto/esperto/demo.pl

8 Conclusions and Future Work

An MT program that offers correct translation of multiwords, either via direct phrasal translation or via paraphrases demonstrates how applied linguistic knowledge helps improve output quality. In this paper, we reassessed the concept of alignment and justified our need for linguistic precision in the alignment task via the analysis of the complexity of multiwords, crucial in obtaining high-quality MT. We, then, described the Logos Model approach to the processing of multiwords and showed how the SemTab function can complement our alignment proxy. We presented the Cross-Lingual Unit Elicitation (CLUE) approach, which is based on the CLUE-Guidelines. These guidelines cover important linguistic phenomena that were left undiscussed in previously presented guidelines. With a special focus on multiwords, we added an extra level to the alignment process, with the hypothesis that this contributes to a deeper scientific process of alignments' annotation. The CLUE-Guidelines led to the gold data set Gold-CLUE, which includes efficiently-aligned non-contiguous multiwords. The linguistic analysis undertaken to establish the Gold-CLUE has allowed some advance in the establishment of a standard for the recognition, processing, translation, and evaluation of multiwords. Some limitations of previous alignment tools (and tasks) motivated the development of the CLUE-Aligner. All alignments were made by using this alignment tool, but only the EN-PT data set was reviewed. We are still in the process of reviewing the remaining language pairs. From the EN-PT Gold-CLUE, we selected which entries would go into the multilingual Paraphrasary, either as simple entries or comment lines for rules. The collection of multilingual paraphrasaries is used in the eSPERTo paraphrase generation system, as exemplified in the paper.

It is important to develop a more robust resource, with a joint discussion of the most challenging linguistic phenomena of the CLUE-Guidelines to improve areas that are known to be non-consensual, a more refined methodology, which supports linguistic phenomena in the four classes identified in this work. All data should be multi-annotated by more than two annotators so that no multiword is left unidentified and the coverage of multiword alignments in the data is complete and there are no disagreements between annotators.

Finally, due to the extent of the work at hand, most linguistic phenomena were left undiscussed. A detailed analysis of these phenomena is important for the improvement of the alignment techniques and for the enhancement of the quality of MT. Our goal is the development of an MT model that integrates linguistic knowledge where all sorts of multiwords are included at the alignment level and feed the paraphrasaries that set into motion and enrich the translation engine.

Acknowledgements

This article was also supported by Fundação para a Ciência e a Tecnologia (FCT), under projects PEst-OE/EEI/LA0021/2011, and also by the EC CIP METANET4U project #270893. We thank the anonymous reviewers for their careful reading of the manuscript, and their insightful and relevant comments and suggestions that helped improve this paper.

References

Baldwin, Timothy and Su Nam Kim. 2010. Multiword Expressions. In Indurkhya, Nitin and Fred J. Damerau, editors, *Handbook of Natural Language Processing, Second Edition*. CRC Press, Taylor and Francis Group, Boca Raton, FL. ISBN 978-1420085921.

Barreiro, Anabela and Fernando Batista. 2016. Machine Translation of Non-Contiguous Multiword Units . In *Proceedings of DiscoNLP 2016* , pages 22 – 30, San Diego, California, June. Association for Computational Linguistics.

Barreiro, Anabela, Annibale Elia, Johanna Monti, and Mario Monteleone. 2010. Mixed up with machine translation: Multi-word units disambiguation challenge. In *Proceedings of the ASLIB Conference: Translating and the Computer*, London, United Kingdom, november.

Barreiro, Anabela, Bernard Scott, Walter Kasper, and Bernd Kiefer. 2011. OpenLogos Rule-Based Machine Translation: Philosophy, Model, Resources and Customization. *Machine Translation*, 25(2):107–126.

Barreiro, Anabela, Johanna Monti, Brigitte Orliac, and Fernando Batista. 2013. When Multiwords Go Bad in Machine Translation. In *Proceedings of the Workshop on Multi-word Units in Machine Translation and Translation Technology, Machine Translation Summit XIV*.

Barreiro, Anabela, Johanna Monti, Brigitte Orliac, Susanne Preuss, Kutz Arrieta, Wang Ling, Fernando

Batista, and Isabel Trancoso. 2014. Linguistic Evaluation of Support Verb Constructions by OpenLogos and Google Translate. In Calzolari, Nicoletta, Khalid Choukri, Thierry Declerck, Hrafn Loftsson, Bente Maegaard, Joseph Mariani, Asuncion Moreno, Jan Odijk, and Stelios Piperidis, editors, *Proceedings of the Ninth International Conference on Language Resources and Evaluation (LREC'14)*, pages 35–40. ELRA.

Barreiro, Anabela, Tiago Luís, and Francisco Raposo. 2016. CLUE-Aligner: An Alignment Tool to Annotate Pairs of Paraphrastic and Translation Units . In *Proceedings of the Tenth International Conference on Language Resources and Evaluation (LREC 2016)*, pages 7–13, Portorož, Slovenia, May. ELRA.

Barreiro, Anabela, Cristina Mota, Jorge Baptista, Lucília Chacoto, and Paula Carvalho. 2022. Linguistic Resources for Paraphrase Generation in Portuguese: a Lexicon-grammar Approach. *Language Resources and Evaluation*, 56(1):1–35, March.

Barreiro, Anabela. 2009. *Make it simple with paraphrases: Automated paraphrasing for authoring aids and machine translation: Universidade do Porto*. Ph.D. thesis, Tese de Doutoramento.

Barreiro, Anabela. 2015. Tradução automática, ma non troppo. *Oslo Studies in Language*, 7(1):207–222.

Brown, Peter F., John Cocke, Stephen Della Pietra, Vincent J. Della Pietra, Frederick Jelinek, John D. Lafferty, Robert L. Mercer, and Paul S. Roossin. 1990. A Statistical Approach to Machine Translation. *Computational Linguistics*, 16(2):79–85.

Butt, Miriam. 2010. The Light Verb Jungle: Still Hacking Away. *Complex Predicates: Cross-Linguistic Perspectives on Event Structure*, 04.

Callison-Burch, Chris and Colin Bannard. 2004. Improving statistical translation through editing. European Association for Machine Translation (EAMT-04) Workshop. In *European Association for Machine Translation*.

Erbach, Gregor and Brigitte Krenn. 1993. Idioms and support-verb constructions in HPSG. Technical Report Report Nr. 28, Computerlinguistik an der Universität des Saarlandes (CLAUS), location=Saarbrücken: Universität des Saarlandes,.

Graça, João, Joana Paulo Pardal, Luísa Coheur, and Diamantino Caseiro. 2008. Building a Golden Collection of Parallel Multi-Language Word Alignment. In Calzolari, Nicoletta, Khalid Choukri, Bente Maegaard, Joseph Mariani, Jan Odjik, Stelios Piperidis, and Daniel Tapias, editors, *Proceedings of the Sixth International Conference on Language Resources and Evaluation (LREC'08)*. ELRA.

Hearne, Mary and Andy Way. 2011. Statistical Machine Translation: A Guide for Linguists and Translators. *Language and Linguistics Compass*, 5(5):205–226.

Jespersen, Otto. 1965. *A modern English grammar on historical principles*. George Allen and Unwin Ltd.

Koehn, Philipp. 2005. EuroParl: A Parallel Corpus for Statistical Machine Translation. In *Conference Proceedings: the tenth Machine Translation Summit*, pages 79–86. AAMT.

Kordoni, Valia and Iliana Simova. 2014. Multiword Expressions in Machine Translation. In Chair), Nicoletta Calzolari (Conference, Khalid Choukri, Thierry Declerck, Hrafn Loftsson, Bente Maegaard, Joseph Mariani, Asuncion Moreno, Jan Odijk, and Stelios Piperidis, editors, *Proceedings of the Ninth International Conference on Language Resources and Evaluation (LREC'14)*, Reykjavik, Iceland, may. European Language Resources Association (ELRA).

Lambert, Patrik, Adrià De Gispert, Rafael Banchs, and José B. Mariño. 2005. Guidelines for Word Alignment Evaluation and Manual Alignment. *Language Resources and Evaluation*, 39(4):267–285.

Maia, Belinda, Rui Sousa Silva, Anabela Barreiro, and Cecília Fróis. 2008. N-grams in search of theories. In Lewandowska-Tomaszczyk, Barbara, editor, *Corpus Linguistics, Computer Tools, and Applications - State of the Art*, volume 17, pages 71–84. Peter Lang.

Orliac, Brigitte and Mike Dillinger. 2003. Collocation extraction for machine translation. In *Proceedings of Machine Translation Summit IX: Papers*, New Orleans, USA, September 23-27.

Scott, Bernard and Anabela Barreiro. 2009. OpenLogos MT and the SAL Representation Language. In Pérez-Ortiz, Juan Antonio, Felipe Sánchez-Martínez, and Francis M. Tyers, editors, *Proceedings of the First International Workshop on Free-Open-Source Rule-Based Machine Translation*, pages 19–26, Alicante, Spain.

Scott, Bernard E. 2003. The Logos Model: An Historical Perspective. *Machine Translation*, 18:1–72.

Scott, Bernard. 2018. *Translation, Brains and the Computer: A Neurolinguistic Solution to Ambiguity and Complexity in Machine Translation*. Springer Publishing Company, Incorporated, 1st edition.

Silberztein, Max. 2003. *NooJ manual*.

Silberztein, Max. 2015. *La formalisation des langues: l'approche NooJ*. Collection science cognitive et management des connaissances. ISTE éd.

Association for Computational Linguistics
209 N. Eighth Street
Stroudsburg, Pennsylvania 18360

ISBN 978-1-7138-8997-7

CURRAN ASSOCIATES INC.
proceedings.com

Second Workshop on Natural Language Interfaces 2023

Nusa Dua, Indonesia
1 November 2023